COLLECTOR'S ENCYCLOPEDIA OF

KNOWLES, TAYLOR & KNOWLES CHINA

identification & values

MARY FRANK GASTON

COLLECTOR BOOKS
A Division Of Schroeder Publishing Co., Inc.

Searching For A Publisher?

We are always looking for knowledgeable people considered to be experts within their fields. If you feel that there is a real need for a book on your collectible subject and have a large comprehensive collection, contact Collector Books.

Other Books by Mary Frank Gaston

The Collector's Encyclopedia of Limoges Porcelain
The Collector's Encyclopedia of R. S. Prussia
The Collector's Encyclopedia of R. S. Prussia, Second Series
The Collector's Encyclopedia of R. S. Prussia, Third Series
The Collector's Encyclopedia of R. S. Prussia, Fourth Series
The Collector's Encyclopedia of Flow Blue China
The Collector's Encyclopedia of Flow Blue China, Second Series
Blue Willow, Revised Second Edition
Art Deco
Antique Brass & Copper

Book Design by Sherry Kraus
Cover Design by Beth Summers

On the Cover:
K. T. & K. (Ohio) Souvenir Plate, $100.00–125.00.
K. T. & K. (Ohio) Pitcher to Wash Set, $100.00–125.00.
K. T. & K. (Ohio) Lotus Ware Vase, $1,800.00–2,000.00.
K. T. & K. (California) Lamb Figurine, $30.00–40.00.
K. T. & K. (California) Pitcher, $45.00–55.00.

Printed by IMAGE GRAPHICS, INC., Paducah, Kentucky

CONTENTS

ACKNOWLEDGMENTS

A number of people contributed photographs and information for this book. I sincerely thank each and every one of those individuals. This book, however, would not have been written without the efforts and encouragement of Nancy and Denver Wetzel. I first met the Wetzels when I was photographing for an article on American Belleek, in 1985. We maintained contact over the following years. They were instrumental in my decision to make a wider range study of the Knowles, Taylor, and Knowles Company than had been possible when I included the company in my book, *American Belleek* (1984). Only a sample of the Wetzel's Lotus Ware was shown in my later article about that china, and over the last nine years, they have added greatly to their collection. The other china made by Knowles, Taylor, and Knowles both before and after Lotus Ware did not come under the scope of that earlier edition.

My husband, Jerry, and I traveled once more to the Wetzel's gracious home in East Liverpool, Ohio, in the spring of 1994. All four of us (plus the Wetzel's beloved dalmatian, Dottie, who showed an avid interest in the goings-on!) worked non-stop to photograph their many examples of Lotus Ware and other china made by the factory. Information and reference materials were also made available to me. Additionally, they introduced me to other collectors who had pieces to contribute to this book. They also photographed some of the china shown. I thank them too for reading a draft of the manuscript and offering comments, corrections, and suggestions.

The Wetzel's also put me in touch with Chris Crain the great-great-grandson of Col. John N. Taylor, one of the company's original owners.

Nancy and Denver Wetzel are native East Liverpoolians. They have had a lifelong interest in the factory which was such an integral part of their city. They are fortunate to have some of the original molds from the factory. Some years ago, Denver was involved in reproducing some of the pieces from those molds at the Pioneer Pottery with the help of that pottery's owners, Lawrence and Mary Howell, and a caster, John Vervin. The new production was marked with Denver Wetzel's and John Vervin's initials.

Mr. Chris Crain of Anaheim, California, has been very helpful in corresponding with me and photographing pieces from his collection. He has generously furnished materials related to the Taylor family and its history. His mother, Patti, was the only daughter of Eileen Taylor from her first marriage. Eileen Taylor was the daughter of Homer J. Taylor, the son of Col. John N. Taylor. Chris has brought to light the handmade California pottery made by his great-grandfather, Homer J. Taylor, during the late 1930s through the late 1940s. I do appreciate his contributions which not only expand the story of Knowles, Taylor, and Knowles, but add a very interesting personal facet as well. I also thank Chris for reading and commenting on the manuscript.

Other contributors include:

Kenneth W. Barney, Olney, Maryland
John Beck, Columbus, Ohio
Margaret Daily, East Liverpool, Ohio
Joseph G. Dunajeski, Hammond, Indiana
Rock Estell, East Liverpool, Ohio
David Mullins, Columbus, Ohio
Jean Riecker, Northville, Michigan
Therman Riggs, East Liverpool, Ohio
Karen and Merle Russo, East Liverpool, Ohio
Linda J. Ryan, Elberta, Alabama

I also thank Mark Twyford, curator of the East Liverpool, Ohio, Ceramic Museum, for permitting me to photograph pieces on display at the Museum.

I thank my husband, Jerry, for photographing many of the pieces shown and for maintaining his interest and help with my books on china.

I thank my publishers, Bill Schroeder and Bill Schroeder, Jr., for supporting me in this study and for continuing to release fine books in beautiful color.

Last, but not least, I thank my editor, Lisa C. Stroup and her staff for all of the fine work accomplished in getting this edition through the many stages of production.

It is my pleasure to dedicate this book to Nancy and Denver Wetzel.

PREFACE

Over the last decade, interest has greatly increased in the china manufactured by early American pottery companies. I focused on one unique aspect of that industry in my book *American Belleek*, published by Collector Books in 1984. The translucent porcelain made by several American companies from the 1890s until the 1930s was discussed and illustrated. One of those companies was Knowles, Taylor & Knowles of East Liverpool, Ohio. That company had been successful in making a translucent china which was called "Belleek" circa 1889. A plant fire, however, was instrumental in causing the company to stop making Belleek porcelain. When the factory was rebuilt, a bone china was made. The company called that china "Lotus Ware." Examples of the Lotus Ware were included in my book on American Belleek because of the company's history of making a Belleek china and their subsequent production of the Lotus Ware which, while not Belleek, was a translucent china and an art ware. The Belleek made by Knowles, Taylor & Knowles is extremely rare, and I was unable to show an example in the book. Several pieces of Lotus Ware were included.

Lotus Ware was also made for only a short period of time, about six years. It, too, is considered scarce and highly collectible. In this book, I am pleased to be able to include a very large assortment of the Lotus Ware production. A few examples of the factory's Belleek porcelain are also shown. While the Belleek and Lotus Ware were the crowning achievements of the Knowles, Taylor & Knowles factory, the company was in business for many years prior to and after that type of china was made.

Commercial china and table wares were the mainstay of the company. This china had an ironstone or semi-vitreous body. Today collectors are interested in these products also as they represent America's early pottery industry, and they also include items of the Victorian era which are not used today and are both interesting and nostalgic.

This book is divided into several sections beginning with a brief history of the company.* Marks used by the factory and pictures of the marks found on examples shown are included. The first set of photographs include a few early examples of the yellow ware and Rockingham ware which were the first types of pottery made by the factory. The Belleek examples are featured in the next section. The largest group of photographs is devoted to the Lotus Ware china.

Following the Lotus Ware pictures are the semi-vitreous wares. These are divided into several categories: Commemorative and Decorative China; Wash Sets and Accessories; Hotel and Table China; and Whiskey Jugs.

The last section of photographs represents an interesting facet of the Knowles, Taylor & Knowles company. Handmade California decorative items made during the 1940s illustrate the work of the Taylor part of the firm in Burbank, California. Homer J. Taylor, the son of John N. Taylor, one of the original partners, moved his family to California after the East Liverpool, Ohio, factory closed during the Depression. A "K. T. & K." mark was incised into the pottery. This pottery is now attracting collector interest.

Some informative and interesting items relating to the company history and production are included in several appendices. Copies of pages from a factory salesman's book show representative lines of Belleek and Lotus Ware china. Illustrations of hotel china and table ware patterns also indicate the wide range made of those items. Photographs of some of the original ceramic molds present a view of an important facet of the manufacturing process. Pictures and documents relating to some members of the John N. Taylor family are also shown.

This value guide lists current price ranges for the china illustrated. Please note that prices are not included for a few items which chiefly relate to the history of the company and which are not available on the secondary market.

Collectors with additional information about the company may write to me. Please include a self-addressed stamped envelope for a reply.

Mary Frank Gaston
P. O. Box 342
Bryan, Texas 77806

*For a detailed historical perspective of the pottery industry including not only the Knowles, Taylor & Knowles Company but also the numerous others which operated in East Liverpool, Ohio, please see the *City of Hills & Kilns* by William C. Gates, Jr.

To Nancy and Denver Wetzel

HISTORY

East Liverpool, Ohio, has been the home of many American potteries since the early 1840s, when an Englishman, James Bennett, found that the area's soil contained the ingredients necessary for making pottery. James Bennett had worked in a pottery in England as a "packer" before he settled in America (*History of Columbiana County Ohio*, 1879: 180). A "packer" would not necessarily know how to make pottery, but evidently James Bennett had absorbed enough of the process to make him feel confident that he could produce articles made of clay. His pottery was financed by some businessmen in East Liverpool, and his first production was in 1840. The type of pottery made was called yellow ware. This is a simple earthenware body which was coated with a yellow glaze. Bennett's pottery was sold to Isaac W. Knowles in 1853, and Bennett moved from East Liverpool to Birmingham, Pennsylvania (*History of Columbiana County Ohio*, 1879: 181).

Knowles and a partner, Isaac A. Harvey, continued to make yellow ware after taking over the factory. They also made Rockingham ware which is a simple clay product covered with a marbled yellow and brown glaze. The yellow ware and Rockingham ware were made as utilitarian products. Simply fashioned mugs, jars, jugs, kettles, plates, and so forth were pieces necessary for storing and serving food during that Victorian period. This type of pottery was not too durable for it was not fired at very high temperatures. Examples from this era are scarce. The East Liverpool, Ohio, Ceramic Museum displays several pieces of yellow ware and Rockingham ware. Some of these are attributed to the early Knowles pottery or are described as being the same type of ware. Evidently marking was not in practice. A few examples photographed at the museum are shown in the first section of photographs.

A *Souvenir* (n.d.) booklet put out by the factory notes that Isaac W. Knowles had a one kiln pottery in 1854. By 1870, there were only two kilns in operation. The growth of the company came about after 1870. Homer S. Knowles, a key figure in the later development of the factory, was Isaac Knowles' son by his first wife. He was born in 1851, only three years prior to his father's purchase of James Bennett's business. Homer worked at the pottery during his youth, and he became interested in the scientific procedures for making china. He became a partner in the company in 1872, along with his brother-in-law, John N. Taylor. Earlier, in 1867, Isaac Knowles had purchased his former partner's (Isaac Harvey) interest n the company (*History of Columbiana County Ohio*, 1879: 179). In 1872, the firm became Knowles, Taylor & Knowles. Two additional partners and family members were brought into the company in 1888. One was Joseph G. Lee, another son-in-law of Isaac Knowles. The other was Willis A. Knowles, Isaac's son from a second marriage. The company was not formally incorporated until 1891.

During the early 1870s, Knowles, Taylor & Knowles was successful in manufacturing a type of china called ironstone or granite ware. This type of pottery was superior to the yellow ware and Rockingham ware. The body was stronger and had a brilliant white vitreous glaze. It was quite durable, but it required materials which were not locally available in East Liverpool. The clays such as kaolin and ball clay were imported from states such as Maine, Missouri, Delaware, and Pennsylvania (*History of Columbiana County Ohio*, 1879: 183). Homer S. Knowles is credited with perfecting the formula for this type of ware for the factory (McCord, 1905: 520).

During the 1870s, the Knowles, Taylor

& Knowles Company thrived due to the manufacturing of this white granite ware. The company ceased producing the yellow wares and Rockingham wares. The factory was enlarged, and by 1879, five kilns were in operation. By 1881, the factory was the largest pottery in America (Gates, 1984: 85). The company produced utilitarian china such as hotel china and table china. The number of kilns had increased to sixteen by the mid to late 1880s.

In addition to growth, improvements in the facilities were also taking place. Isaac Knowles was an inventor, and he was able to make technical advances in the pottery making process. Cox (1940) notes that he invented a shaft-driven jigger which was the first machinery introduced into an American pottery. Previously, all of the production processes were by hand. Knowles' inventions were patented and were adapted into use by other factories.

The company also had its own electric plant which furnished the light which was so necessary for the workers. The electric plant made it possible to have elevators and electric fans as well. A private railroad connected parts of the plant and served also to connect the factory to the Pennsylvania rail system. This enabled materials to be brought in for making the granite ware and also provided the means to distribute the finished products. A private telephone system connected the various parts of the plant, and a forge, machine shop, and woodworking shop were also located on the premises (*Souvenir*, n.d).

While the factory was indeed growing and it could adequately produce utilitarian china, the owners were more ambitious. They, like several other American pottery manufacturers in the Trenton, New Jersey, area, wanted to make a very fine china which was not thick and opaque like the iron stone, but thin and translucent. Their goal was to emulate the artistic china made by factories such as the Royal Worcester Company in England and the Belleek factory in Ireland.

The knowledge and expertise for making that type of china were not available in America. It was necessary to hire workers from Ireland and England to come to this country to teach them how to make the body paste and glazes. The techniques and recipes were not written down in books accessible to anyone who might be interested. Historically, porcelain making was shrouded in secrecy after true, translucent china was first made in Europe at the famous German Meissen factory in the early 1700s. Pottery owners from that time on in other areas really had little trouble in persuading workers to leave one factory and come to another to reveal the secret processes. Consequently, true or hard paste porcelain manufacturing spread to other parts of Europe and eventually to America.

Knowles, Taylor & Knowles was very successful in obtaining a very knowledgeable person, Joshua Poole, to implement the porcelain making process for the East Liverpool, Ohio, factory. Poole had been the manager of the Irish Belleek factory. He came to work for Knowles, Taylor & Knowles in 1887 (Cox, 1938). Poole, with the help of Homer S. Knowles, worked on developing a china body similar to the Irish Belleek.

The Irish Belleek was not a bone china. The Belleek body was also not the same as hard paste or true porcelain, although it was made from the same type of ingredients. The method of manufacturing was different in that the Belleek body became vitreous (like glass with an impenetrable body) and translucent in one firing. The body of the ware was called "parian" after the first firing, and it was unglazed. Glazes were added later and the ware was refired. Hard paste porcelain, however, becomes translucent during the first firing, but it does not become vitreous until the bisque (first baked body) is coated with a glaze and then refired. During this second firing at extremely high temperature, the glaze and body literally melt together, making the piece vitreous and non-pourous. When the glaze is applied to the Belleek parian body and refired, the glaze does not melt into the body because the body is already impenetrable or non-pourous.

The glaze on the Belleek body actually acts as a separate coating. The unique Irish Belleek glazes became the distinctive characteristics of the china because they were lustrous and iridescent like pearls. It is especially important for fine china to have a vitreous or non-pourous body so that the china does not crackle or craze. China which is not vitreous will craze and often discolor over time.

A new factory or plant was built by Knowles, Taylor & Knowles for the production of fine china during 1888. It was called the China Works (Cox, 1952: 1). Production was begun for the Belleek body perfected at the factory sometime during 1888. Undated pages from a company catalog show an assortment of items which were made. Tea sets, shell dishes, pitchers, a lily form vase, and a gipsy kettle were some examples.

Unfortunately, the new plant was destroyed by fire from a gas explosion in 1888. Production of the K.T.&K. Belleek lasted only a few months. The factory was swiftly rebuilt in less than a year. The production of Belleek china, however, was halted. While the attempt to make a translucent china had been successful, the manufacturing process was too costly.

The Belleek china produced during that very short period of time was marked with the K.T&K. logo and "Belleek." Because of the limited production, examples of K.T.&K.'s Belleek china are extremely rare. A tea set with the mark is shown in the photographs along with three other unmarked examples. A copy of the catalog page illustrating pieces from the Belleek production is shown in the appendices.

After the plant was rebuilt in 1889, the company continued to manufacture utilitarian granite ware for commercial use and semi-vitreous ware for table and household use. Knowles, Taylor & Knowles did not give up their goal, however, to make a fine, artistic type of china. This time, the aim was to produce a china body which would be somewhat less fragile than the Belleek body. Experiments were made with bone china which uses the ash from the calcined bones of animals as the major ingredient

in the ceramic body paste. This type of china was being made in England. With the expertise of Joshua Poole and Homer S. Knowles, a type of bone china with a beautiful lustrous glaze was developed at the K.T.&K. factory.

Other Englishmen were imported by the company to design and execute the production of this newly invented china. In 1889, a designer and decorator from the Royal Worcester factory was hired, and Kenneth P. Beattie became the chief modeler (Frelinghuysen, 1989: 212, 216). William and George Morely, who were also connected with the Staffordshire pottery industry, were hired as decorators (Cox, 1938). These two men were uncle and nephew respectively. They were not brothers as some thought because the two men were about the same age. Eventually the Morleys left East Liverpool and worked as artists for the Lenox factory in Trenton, New Jersey. That company was also engaged in making a Belleek type of china (Robinson and Feeny, 1980: 42).

The bone china body perfected at the Knowles, Taylor & Knowles factory was named "Lotus Ware." That name was incorporated into a mark on the ware. It is said that the name was chosen because the first vase made was decorated with floral shapes designed after the lotus blossom (Lehner, 1980). A lotus blossom is featured on top of the Lotus Ware mark.

Lotus Ware was designed as an art porcelain. Graceful body shapes, often exhibiting Art Nouveau influences, were made. Catalog pages circa 1893 indicate that the company also devised elaborate names for the various shapes of ewers, pitchers, and vases. Many of these were based on terms identified with early civilizations in Europe and the Middle East. Roman, Greco, Umbrian, Etruscan, Egyptian, and Luxor are some examples. Some designs also showed the influence of the Irish Belleek shapes in the form of naturalistic themes with twig and branch styled handles and subjects from marine life such as shells and coral.

The Lotus Ware made during the early 1890s did indeed live up to the goal of the owners of Knowles, Taylor & Knowles. The china proved that the company could make a ceramic body equal to the finest made in Europe. Knowles, Taylor & Knowles received the top awards for the Lotus Ware at the 1893 World's Exhibition in Chicago. This was quite a feat for the extremely brief amount of time that the company had been engaged in making the ware.

Other distinctive decorations associated with Lotus Ware were designed and chiefly implemented by Henry Schmidt. Sometime in 1893, Schmidt, a German, came to work at the factory to create his unique applied decoration to the Lotus Ware china. He is noted to have previously worked at the Meissen factory (Frelinghuysen, 1989: 215). He came to America and worked in New York City and Trenton, New Jersey, before he was hired at Knowles, Taylor & Knowles (Blake, 1938).

Blake, cited above, became Schmidt's assistant at the factory. Much of the information concerning Schmidt's work which has been handed down through the years is based on Will T. Blake's letter in 1938 to Lucille Cox, an early researcher of the factory's history and production of Lotus Ware. Schmidt is said to have worked in secrecy and to have had little association with the other factory employees. He did not speak English, and that is one reason Blake was designated to be his assistant. Blake could help Schmidt with his English and also learn his techniques in case Schmidt was not available (for whatever reason) to decorate the china (Blake, 1938).

Schmidt dressed in pastel colored smocks and was considered to be an artist at the factory (Cox, 1952: 1). He had developed a method of applying decoration to china by using a tube-like instrument to squeeze liquid china paste onto the china body in the form of flowers and leaves and intricate open-work designs. "Filigreed" is the term used by the factory in the Lotus Ware catalog to describe the open-work decoration. "Fishnet," "Fish Scale," "Jewels," or "Jewelling" are also descriptive words used by collectors to refer to some of the applied designs.

The Lotus Ware Mark consisted of a crescent moon shape within a circle with the initials "K. T. & K." A Lotus blossom was placed at the top of the circle. A variation of the mark used the full company name rather than initials. Another mark of "K. T. & K." over "CHINA" was also used on the Lotus Ware production. Barber, (1893: 109) indicated that the KT&K/CHINA mark was placed on white porcelain, meaning undecorated china; the Lotus Ware mark was reserved for factory decorated porcelain. Evidently, the practice, if that was in fact the intent of the company, was not consistent. Factory decorated examples are also found with the KT&K/CHINA mark. The KT&K/CHINA mark, however, is more frequently found on non-porcelain items. Sometimes, however, the shapes of the non-porcelain items are the same as some of the porcelain pieces. The same molds were used for both porcelain and non-porcelain items in some cases.

Boger (1978) states that the factory-decorated pieces included the artist's initial and the date decorated. Some examples do have both initials and dates, but many factory-decorated pieces do not. It is evident that the Lotus Ware porcelain, whether marked with a Lotus Ware mark or a KT&K/CHINA mark is often found with non-factory and non-professional decoration. Sometimes, such pieces have names, years, or initials painted on the bases: "J. M. J. Xmas 95" for example. Such bold signatures as well as the quality of the handpainted work are usually the chief clues that the piece was not decorated at the factory.

Hand-painted china was a popular hobby and business during the late 1800s and early 1900s. While china painting was often a pastime for young women, men also painted china. Professional decorating studios were formed across the country for the purpose of decorating blanks which were then sold to the public. The Illinois based Pickard studio is one of the most famous. Blanks or undecorated china were a big business for European china companies, and Knowles, Taylor & Knowles also took advantage of that growing market. The factory is noted to have produced a large amount of undecorated china. The catalog pages showing Lotus Ware indicate "white" in the descriptions of some of the styles shown. Others are obviously unpainted. (See these catalog pages in the appendices.) Thus , it is apparent that many pieces would have been decorated outside the factory. Non-factory decorated Lotus Ware must be judged on the quality of the hand-painted decoration. Some is quite good and professional in appearance. Others, however, are not. Poorly decorated examples were usually just painted and not refired. They have what is known as a "cold" or "raw" finish. Other non-factory decorated pieces, however, have been refired because it was not uncommon for china painters, especially those more skilled in the art, to have their own kiln where the decoration could be refired and thus exhibit a more professional appearance. All Lotus Ware is considered scarce, and thus values are usually high regardless of the quality of the decoration. Professionally decorated pieces, however, command the premium prices.

The history of Lotus Ware was not a long one. This fine translucent china with the beautiful smooth glaze was manufactured for only about six years, from circa 1889 (Cox, 1952) until about 1896. A brief attempt was made in 1904 for a few months to resume this type of production, but it was soon discontinued (*Echoes*, 1989). The production was too costly, and the American market continued to prefer foreign-made china notably from England, France, and Germany. Knowles, Taylor & Knowles knew that it must drop this line of china if the company was to survive.

After 1906, the factory reverted to producing semi-vitreous china with a large part of the output geared to the commercial market. China was made for various hotels and clubs as well as for rail and steamship lines. Commemorative and souvenir china was also made for clubs and fraternal organizations. A page from a catalog illustrates examples of the types of various logos and names that a company or organization could choose to have china custom made. The catalog notes that the

monograms, crests, names, and so forth were available in the underglaze colors of dark blue, peacock, black, red, brown, dark brown, gray, and French green. These same colors were also available in a selection of dinner ware patterns composed chiefly of transfer printed floral border designs.

For collectors, examples of the commercial china are chiefly found in a few categories. One would be commemorative items for clubs and organizations. These pieces may be decorated with some historical theme or figure. Sometimes the specific name of the historical event or subject is printed on the piece. The name of the club or organization is often printed on the back, sometimes with a lengthy description. See an example in KT&K Mark 7. Other decorative china which has transfer decoration would be included in this first category such as portrait plates and vases with floral or figural themes. Included with these decorative semi-vitreous pieces In the photographs are several items decorated by Alf Potter, a Knowles, Taylor & Knowles factory artist. These pieces probably represent the prime artistic examples of the semi-vitreous wares, ranking Just under the Lotus Ware in desirability for collectors.

A second collectible category comprises items unique to the Victorian household or hotel such as pieces to wash sets, vanities, and spittoons. Table wares such as pitchers, mugs, syrup or molasses cans, cracker jars, and mustard pots are some other popular items. Dinner ware patterns may also interest collectors who might have inherited pieces or partial sets. Children's china such as the tea set shown in the photographs and one in the appendices from an advertisement are highly sought by collectors.

A third collectible KT&K category is whiskey jugs. These were made by the factory from the late 1800s through the late 1920s. The company made jugs for various whiskey manufacturers, distillers, and distributors. The company was able to use the transfer decorating technique to put whatever name, brand, or logo on the jug the buyer might desire. The jugs were marked with the

KT&K/CHINA mark. They have a fine white body glaze. They were made in half-pint, pint, and quart sizes and were distinguished by a serpent shaped handle. These jugs were known as "Presentation Jugs" because they were used by the whiskey distributors as gifts for special customers or for special occasions (Sullivan, 1992). Sullivan notes that on some examples where there is a date such as "Meredith Diamond Club Pure Rye 1880," that the date indicates the time when the whiskey was made, not the jug.

A number of names of distributors will be found on the jugs. One of the most frequently found is that of "Meredith." George W. Meredith founded his company in East Liverpool, Ohio. He had been a jiggerman at the KT&K factory before he started blending liquors to make his own brand of whiskey (Popp, 1973). He commissioned Knowles, Taylor & Knowles to make jugs for him. Additionally, he ordered some miniature jugs, 1½" high, made for an extra form of advertising. These were used as fobs or charms for men's watches.

In addition to the whiskey jugs decorated with specific distributor's names and brands, collectors are interested in the same type of jugs which have hand-painted decorations. It is probable that many of the jugs were sold as white ware and were decorated outside the factory. Some of the hand-painted decoration is quite professional in appearance and other decoration is not, the same as Lotus Ware. Some of the jugs have transfer designs, and some are even found with sterling silver overlay which would have been applied by some silver manufacturer. Silver decorated china was popular for a time in the early 1900s, and such examples today are very collectible. Some of the whiskey jugs, however, clearly show, if one looks closely, that the hand-painted work was applied directly over the whiskey distributor's name and brand! Like other hand-painted china, the quality of the painting is the key factor in determining value. A selection of whiskey distributors' jugs and handpainted jugs is shown in the photographs.

There is no doubt that the Lotus Ware years were the height of excellence for the company and coincided also with the peak of the American porcelain industry itself. Although the factory continued in business for over 30 years after Lotus Ware production had been discontinued, the company relied on commercial china and table wares to stay in business. Knowles, Taylor & Knowles, like other American porcelain manufacturers, fell victim to the imported china from abroad, particularly that from Japan during the 1920s. Paris (1990: 41) notes that by 1928, Japan was supplying over 60 percent of the imported china to the United States. The Depression was another factor in the demise of the American china factories. From having been the largest china factory in the country, Knowles, Taylor & Knowles effectively closed in 1929. At that time, the company became one of eight factories which was combined to form the American China Corporation (Lehner, 1978: 48). That corporation's production stopped in 1931 when bankruptcy was declared. The buildings which had housed the Knowles, Taylor & Knowles Company were demolished in 1935 (Gates, 1984: 314, 315).

By the time the company closed, its founders had died. Isaac W. Knowles died in 1902. His son-in-law and partner, John Neely Taylor died in 1914 (Crain, 1994). Isaac's son, Homer S. Knowles, died at the age of 41 in 1892, ten years prior to the death of his father (McCord, 1905: 162).

Homer's son, Harold Homer Knowles, born in 1884, became active in the East Liverpool factory about 1901 (McCord, 1905: 521). He later became manager (Evans, 1978: 33). Perhaps foreseeing the end of the East Liverpool factory, Harold Homer opened a pottery factory in Santa Clara, California, in 1923. He had incorporated the company in 1920 in Delaware with two partners from Los Angeles. Construction of the plant started in 1921. When the factory opened n 1923, it had the capacity to employ about 350 people. The company was able to remain in business for only about five months, however, before it declared bankruptcy. During its short duration, the factory made table china and some art ware. The marks were incised and consisted of "K. T. & K." with or without "Calif." (Evans, 1978: 34). Lehner (1988: 238) notes the same marks as Evans with a slight variation being "K. T. K. of California." Lehner also shows a stamped mark consisting of a tree with "Orchard Ware by Knowles" printed inside the top of the tree shape. Presumably, this mark would have been on table ware. Lehner additionally indicates that the Santa Clara factory used an incised mark of "K. T. & K. Hand Made California." This particular mark, however, has probably been erroneously attributed to the 1920s Santa Clara factory. It was the mark used by a Burbank, California, pottery during the late 1930s through the late 1940s. This later pottery also had, however, a direct connection to the Knowles, Taylor & Knowles Company of East Liverpool, Ohio.

The Burbank pottery was founded by Homer J. Taylor, the son of John N. Taylor, one of the original partners of Knowles, Taylor & Knowles. Homer J. Taylor became president of the Ohio business when his father, John Neely Taylor died on October 21, 1914. Homer J. Taylor moved his family to California in 1934 after the East Liverpool factory closed. His family included his wife, Pearl, and his children, Eileen, Bonnie, and John. The original site of the Burbank pottery was at 1209 Chestnut Street. It was housed in what had previously been a chicken coop. The chicken coop was 24 feet wide and 80 feet long, and was one of four such buildings. The Taylors rented only one at first for $10.00 a month. Later, they were able to expand to the other buildings. Family members were active in the production, and some pieces were initialed or signed by them. The company was in business for a little over ten years, circa 1937 to 1948 (Crain, 1994).

A variety of decorative ceramic pieces for the home were made. Bowls, flower floaters, vases, wall pockets, and novelty items such as planters in the form of boots, roosters, or ducks are some of the items. The glazes are the chief distinction of the wares. Many have a mottled look made by dipping the pieces in one color of glaze and then spraying the piece with a different color (Crain, 1994). Dark blue was a favorite color as was a wine or raspberry shade. A chartreuse finish indicates the color fads of the late 1940s. The china was marked with the incised letters "K. T. & K." and "Calif." "Hand Made" was also often included.

The examples clearly illustrate that the pottery was hand made; hence the use of "Hand Made" in the marks. Lack of examples from the earlier Santa Clara pottery makes it difficult to say with certainty that it did not also use "hand made" in its marks, but it is reasonable to suggest that lack of knowledge about the Burbank pottery may account for pieces with those incised words being incorrectly attributed to the 1923 Santa Clara factory. No references on American pottery marks or companies include the Burbank pottery. The information presented here was furnished by Chris Crain, the great-grandson of Homer J. Taylor, the founder of the Burbank pottery.

The last section of photographs in this book illustrates the Burbank production. Like other American, and especially California pottery, which is fifty or more years old, collector interest in these pieces is mounting. Unfortunately, due probably to the short period of production of the earlier Santa Clara pottery, only one example, possibly from that company, is shown.

The last photograph is a vase with the design of a bird in relief on the front. The overall nature of this piece is unlike the other pieces illustrated which are attributed to the Burbank pottery. The vase has an incised mark of "K. T. K." over "Calif." The mark itself, is also noted to be somewhat more precisely or evenly made than the marks found on the other items. Hopefully, pieces will surface in the future which can be attributed definitely to the Santa Clara pottery. Collectors will be interested in these pieces, as well as those shown from the Burbank pottery, not only for their inherent collectibility but also for their link to the Knowles, Taylor & Knowles factory of East Liverpool, Ohio.

MARKS

The East Liverpool factory used a variety of back stamps over the course of its operations. Although the company was started in 1854, the earliest mark appears to date from the early 1870s, a time which reflects the company's production of ironstone china. Gates and Ormerod (1982: 10, 116) show a coat of arms mark with "Iron Stone China" printed above and "K. T. & K." printed below, used circa 1872 to 1878. The first patented mark was a Buffalo or Bison trademark which was patented in 1878 (Gates and Ormerod, 1982: 10).

Barber (1904: 108, 109) listed 34 marks used by Knowles, Taylor & Knowles prior to 1904. He only dated a few, however, and those were after 1870. Eighteen of the marks shown by Barber were in the form of banners with the names of states, cities, and universities. He noted that such marks were used by the company to identify specific shapes and patterns. These included "Iowa," "Detroit," and "Yale" for example. Subsequent books on American china marks usually include these same particular marks. Examples bearing such marks are not frequently found. Gates and Ormerod (1982: 122–124) indicate that many of these marks were used circa mid 1880s to early 1900s. Lehner (1978: 48; 1988; 238, 239) illustrates several other marks, but few are dated.

Collectors are referred to two references for specific and detailed information regarding marks used by Knowles, Taylor & Knowles: *The East Liverpool, Ohio, Pottery District*, 1982 by William C. Gates, Jr. and Dana E. Ormerod; and *DeBolt's Dictionary of American Marks*, 1994, by Gerald DeBolt. I have based the dates for the marks shown in this book, which are found on illustrated pieces, on the dating periods shown by DeBolt. His marks are divided into categories such as Buffalo, Eagle, and name and initial marks. A simple chart lists the various types of marks and their dating periods as shown by DeBolt. Where one of the marks is like one shown in this book, I have indicated my mark number to show an example of the mark. The KT&K marks in this book are numbered 1 through 11a. These numbers are used for the purpose of identifying which mark was found on a particular piece of china shown in the photographs. The mark numbers are not DeBolt's; he does not number the marks in his reference. The marks shown in the marks section here also do not include all of the marks and variations of those marks which were used by the factory over the course of its history.

Type of Mark	Debolt's Dating Periods	Gaston Mark Numbers
Coat of Arms Mark	1872–1878	no example
Buffalo or Bison Marks	1878 – 1885	Mark 1
Eagle Marks		
with Iron Stone China	1880–1890	Mark 2
with Shield and Iron Stone China	1880–1890	Marks 3 and 3a
with Shield and Trade Mark	1880–1885	Mark 4 (without Belleek and in dark green)
with Shield and Belleek	1889	Mark 4
with Circle and Semi-Vitreous Porcelain	1890–1907	Mark 7
variation of this mark	1897	Mark 8
variation of this mark	1900	Mark 9
Lotus Ware Mark	1890s	Mark 6
Initial Marks		
K. T. & K./CHINA	1890–1905	Mark 5
K. T. & K./S—V/CHINA	after 1905	Mark 10
K. T. & K./S—V/IVORY	late 1920s	Mark 11 and 11a

DeBolt has been able to decode the KT&K dating system for some of the marks used about 1900 and after. Some of the marks discussed above such as the Eagle Semi-Vitreous Mark (see mark 9) and the KT&K/S—V/CHINA mark (see mark 10) may sometimes be found with either numbers, letters, or a combination of numbers and letters beneath the mark. According to DeBolt (1994: 76, 77), the last digit of a group of 3 numbers or last two digits of a group of 4 numbers indicates the year the item was made. The dating method appears to have been used for the Eagle mark from 1900 to 1915 and for the KT&K/S—V/CHINA mark from 1905 to 1915. (For elaboration on this system, see DeBolt, 1994: 76, 77.)

DeBolt surmises that the Eagle mark was discontinued about 1914. A group of three letters was used with the KT&K/S—V/CHINA mark after 1915 until 1926 with the last letter signifying the year. "A" would stand for 1915. In 1927, the factory reverted back to numbers with the middle two digits of a four number group showing the year (see mark 10). After 1927, letters and numbers were combined with the letter indicating the year. For that system, the letter "A" would equal 1928. this last dating code was not in use too long since the company closed in 1929.

The KT&K Ohio marks are found on pages 19–20. The KT&K California marks are included with the photographs of that china in the last section of pictures.

I.
KNOWLES, TAYLOR & KNOWLES
OHIO

Marks

Yellow Ware and Rockingham Ware

Ironstone or Granite Ware

Belleek Porcelain

Lotus Ware

Semi-Vitreous Ware

Commemorative and Decorative China

Wash Sets and Accessories

Hotel and Table China

Whiskey Jugs

Marks

KT&K Mark 1, Buffalo or Bison Mark, ca. 1878–1885.

KT&K Mark 2, Eagle with "Iron Stone China" and "Knowles, Taylor and Knowles," ca. 1880–1890.

KT&K Mark 3, Eagle in Shield with "Iron Stone China" and "Knowles, Taylor and Knowles, Patented," ca. 1880–1890.

KT&K Mark 3a, the same as Mark 3 without "Patented." Other variations of Mark 3 have the initials "K. T. & K." rather than the company name spelled in full.

KT&K Mark 4, this mark is similar to Mark 3a, except it includes "Trade Mark" and "K. T. & K." initials. This mark has "Belleek" printed under the Eagle and Shield emblem, and the mark is printed in purple, ca. 1889.

KT&K Mark 5, "K. T. & K." initials over "CHINA," ca. 1890–1905. This mark is found on both Lotus Ware bodies (translucent china) and semi-vitreous china (opaque bodies).

KT&K Mark 6, Lotus Ware printed outside a circle with the initials "K. T. & K." printed inside the circle; the mark may also appear with the company name spelled in full rather than in initial form, ca. 1889–1896.

KT&K Mark 7, Eagle within a Circle with "Semi-Vitreous Porcelain" printed inside the circle. There is a KTK monogram on top of the circle, and "Knowles, Taylor & Knowles" is printed around the outer ring. "East Liverpool, Ohio, U. S. A." is printed below the circle, ca. 1890–1907. This mark also includes an example of the special marking the factory applied for china made exclusively for various clubs and organizations.

KT&K Mark 9, this is another variation of the Eagle and Circle Mark with "Semi-Vitreous Porcelain" printed around the outer ring of the circle and "K. T. & K." printed beneath the mark, ca. 1900–1915. This type of mark may sometimes have a group of 3 or 4 numbers under the company name indicating year of manufacture, see DeBolt, 1994: 74.

KT&K Mark 8, similar to Mark 7, except this is a simpler version with only an Eagle and "Semi-Vitreous" printed inside the circle and "Porcelain" printed at the base of the circle, ca. 1897.

KT&K Mark 10, "K. T. & K." initials over "S—V" over "CHINA," ca. after 1905 through the 1920s. This mark may also be found with a group of 3 or 4 numbers or letters indicating year of manufacture, (see DeBolt, 1994: 74, 75). This example has 4 numbers with the middle two "27" indicating the year 1927. In the captions of the photographs, Mark 10 only refers to the mark without numbers unless otherwise noted.

KT&K Mark 11, "K. T. & K." initials over "S—V" over "IVORY," ca. 1920s. This mark is similar to Mark 10 and has a variation which does not include the "S—V." Mark 11 may also be found with a dating code, see DeBolt, 1994: 75.

KT&K Mark 11a, variation of Mark 11, "K. T & K." over "IVORY" ca. late 1920s.

Yellow Ware and Rockingham Ware

Yellow ware Bowl similar to the yellow ware pottery made by the early Knowles factory. Unpriced.
Collection of the East Liverpool Museum of Ceramics.

Yellow ware Tea Kettles decorated with hand-painted floral decor, attributed to Knowles, Taylor & Knowles, circa 1871. Unpriced.
Collection of the East Liverpool Museum of Ceramics.

Rockingham ware Canning Jar with wine seal and Rockingham ware Cuspidor, similar to the Rockingham ware made by Knowles, Taylor & Knowles in the 1870s. Unpriced.
Collection of the East Liverpool Museum of Ceramics.

Ironstone or Granite Ware

Open-handled Platter, 12¾" l x 9" w, dark cobalt blue outer border; hand-painted scene of the figure of a drape- clad woman with a fan, a hat, and a parasol wading in a pond, decorates center; rare item; KT&K Mark 1. $400.00–500.00.
Crain Collection.

Vase, approximately 6" h, cylinder shape, hand-painted decoration of a wide maroon band with narrow gold bands; Buffalo trademark (similar to Mark 1). $225.00–275.00.
East Liverpool Museum of Ceramics Collection.

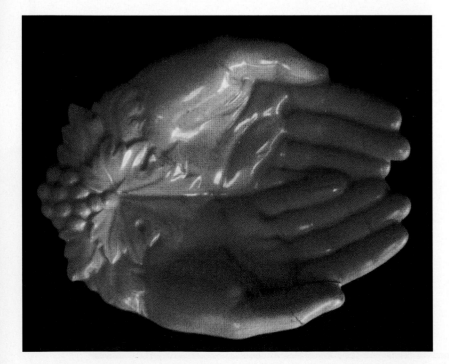

Molded Hands with grapes and leaves in relief. The hands of Belle Taylor, wife of Col. John N. Taylor, served as the original mold for the hands. The hands were noted to have been copied both in pottery and glass (Crain, 1994); KT&K Mark 2; rare item.
Unpriced.
Crain Collection.

Plate, 8¾" d, pattern of white dogwood blossoms on a dark blue background, KT&K Mark 3a.
$75.00–100.00.
Estell Collection.

Pitcher, 12" h, KT&K Mark 3a; the same white dogwood pattern as shown in the preceding picture decorates this piece; the dark pink background covers the top two-thirds of the body; a basket weave pattern is visible on the undecorated lower body.
$100.00–150.00
Estell Collection.

Pitcher with molded spout and hinged metal spout cover and lid; a multicolored bird with flowering branches is painted on the front; the reverse of this pitcher has a brown-tone winter scene as shown in the next picture.
$1,500.00–1,800.00.
East Liverpool Museum of Ceramics Collection.

Pitcher, 11½" h, brown-tone winter scene, KT&K Mark 3; there is no decoration on the reverse side of this pitcher.
$1,200.00–1,500.00.
Estell Collection.

Cup and Saucer decorated with a Moss Ross design, ironstone, circa 1872 to1890. $75.00–100.00.
East Liverpool Museum of Ceramics Collection.

Mustache Cup with pink glaze and white floral branch and "Present" in relief decorating exterior, ironstone, circa 1872 to 1890. $150.00–200.00.
East Liverpool Museum of Ceramics Collection.

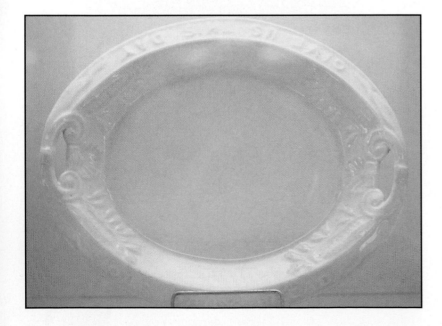

Bread Platter with molded floral work around border, ironstone, circa 1872 to 1890. $175.00–225.00.
East Liverpool Museum of Ceramics Collection.

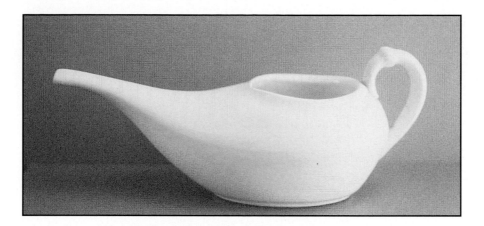

Invalid Feeder, ironstone, circa 1872 to 1890.
(Identified as a pitcher, but usually this type of piece is called an invalid feeder.)
$125.00–150.00.
East Liverpool Museum of Ceramics Collection

Tea Set, probably a child's or individual "morning set" because of small size, simple gold band or wedding ring decor, ironstone, circa 1872 to 1890.
$600.00–800.00 set.
East Liverpool Museum of Ceramics Collection.

Teapot, metal lid, blue bird decor, ironstone, circa 1872 to 1890.
$250.00–300.00
East Liverpool Museum of Ceramics Collection.

Belleek
Porcelain

Tea Set: Teapot (#89), 4" h; Creamer (#87), 2½" h; Covered Sugar Bowl (#88), 3½" h; the numbers are company catalog numbers for the Belleek production. The ribbed body design was named Melon. The body surface has a pebbled texture, and the creamy color of the glaze is quite similar to the Irish Belleek; gold trim; KT&K Mark 4. The catalog illustrates a tea cup and saucer and an after dinner cup and saucer in this design as well; a marked three piece Tea Set in the Belleek porcelain is quite rare, and this example is the only known existing one.
$8,000.00–10,000.00 set.
Wetzel Collection.

Creamer, Belleek body, Melon design, attributed to being similar to KT&K Belleek in the Museum description; the piece is the same as the Creamer in the preceding Tea Set, except there is no gold trim.
$1,500.00–2,000.00.
East Liverpool Museum of Ceramics Collection.

Tusk Jugs, 7¼" h, unmarked, attributed to Belleek wares which survived the factory fire in 1889 and were later decorated. The catalog page for Belleek shows four sizes of the Tusk Jug, #106. The shape is similar to one made by the Royal Worcester Factory in England. These examples are decorated with a green glaze on the upper body and stenciled work in the form of a middle border and wheat designs on the lower body.
$1,500.00–2,000.00 each.
Wetzel Collection.

Teapot, decorated with white bands punctuated with gold bead work on a dark blue body glaze; unmarked, but attributed to Belleek ware.
$1,500.00–2,000.00.
Wetzel Collection.

Lotus Ware

The china shown in this section represents the translucent Lotus Ware china. All pieces have Mark 6 unless otherwise noted. A few items have Mark 5 (KT&K/CHINA) because some of the translucent china was also marked with Mark 5 rather than the Lotus Ware Mark. A Shell Dish is shown which incorporates both Mark 5 and Mark 6, illustrating the use of Mark 5 on a Lotus Ware body. The mark is shown with the dish. The Lotus Ware china is presented here in several sections.

The first includes:

Bon-bons

Bowls

Compote

Chocolate Jugs

Cracker Jars

Tea Sets

Shaving Mug

Leaf Bon-bon Dish, catalog #243, 6" h x 7½" d, three feet fashioned in the form of floral buds with a matching applied design on lid. The mold is delicately veined to exhibit the characteristics of a leaf; the lid has an upturned crimped border.
$3,000.00–3,500.00.
Wetzel Collection.

Bon Nappie, catalog #260, footed, 8"1 ; decorated with an enameled floral design in turquoise and gold. The catalog indicates that these dishes also were made in a 5½" and a 6½" size.
$300.00-350.00.
Wetzel Collection.

Finger Bowl, 2¾" h x 5¼" d, catalog #258; gold sponged work on ruffled border.
$150.00–200.00.
Wetzel Collection.

Oatmeal Nappie, catalog #263, 2" h x 5½" d; hand-painted floral design highlighted by pink roses around inner and outer border and in center of bowl, gold trim.
$200.00–250.00.
Wetzel Collection.

Oatmeal Nappie, catalog #263,
2" h x 5½" d, undecorated.
$175.00–225.00.
Wetzel Collection.

Orange Dish, catalog #266, 3½" h x 11½" 1; transfer
decor of small pink roses with gold highlighting
some of the embossed mold designs.
$300.00–400.00.
Wetzel Collection.

Bowl, 3" h, 10" d, swirl mold design finished with an
iridescent pearlized glaze; a transfer portrait of a
Victorian woman is shown on the interior of the bowl.
$1,000.00–1,200.00.
Wetzel Collection.

Compote, 6" h x 10" d, pedestal base; light blue
finish around top border with a pink and blue floral
design scattered around interior of bowl.
$500.00–600.00.
Wetzel Collection.

Chocolate Jug, 9" h, catalog #208,
Quincy design; KT&K Mark 5;
gold paste floral decor.
$700.00–800.00.
Wetzel Collection.

Chocolate Jug, 9" h, catalog #208,
Quincy design with After Dinner Coffee Cup, 2½" h,
and Saucer, 5" d, Mecca design, catalog #228.
These two pieces are from a set which includes five cups
and saucers each with a different
hand-painted floral design, non-factory decoration.
Cup and Saucer, $75.00–100.00.
Chocolate Jug, $400.00–500.00.
Wetzel Collection.

Cracker Jar, 7½" h, catalog
#226; fishnet and beaded
work decorate alternate
panels of jar.
$500.00–600.00.
Wetzel Collection.

Chocolate Jug, 9" h, catalog #231, Winona design; this jug has
the same shape as Quincy, #208, but the body design is different
and consists of embossed floral work, undecorated.
$500.00–600.00.
Wetzel Collection.

Cracker Jar, catalog #225; a cream glaze is enhanced by a light pink tint at base with gold sponged work around top border; KT&K Mark 5; $400.00–500.00.
Dunajeski Collection.

Plate, 8½" d, scalloped border, flat base similar to that of a tea tile, undecorated, rare item. $200.00–300.00.
Wetzel Collection.

Tea Set: Pot, 4½" h x 7" w; Covered Sugar Bowl, 4½" h x 5½" w; Creamer, 3¼" h x 4½" w; catalog #246, Valenciennes design; fishnet work painted gold showing white body with a light cream colored matte finish on the smooth parts of the body; the handles of all pieces and interior rim of the teapot have a light green matte finish, non-factory decoration.
$900.00–1,000.00 set.
Wetzel Collection.

Tea Set, catalog #206, Venice design; hand-painted pink flowers alternate with panels of gold vertical lines, heavy gold trim, non-factory decoration; base of pieces initialed "HWM from IAM" and "January 1st 1894." $600.00–700.00 set.
Wetzel Collection.

Tea Set: Teapot, 5" h x 8" w; Covered Sugar Bowl, 4½" h x 6" w; Creamer, 3" h x 4¼" w; small pink and blue floral panels alternate with light blue painted panels; pieces are distinguished by wide gold floral border designs, gold outlining on panels, and gold finish on handles and finials, non-factory decoration.
$600.00–700.00 set.
Wetzel Collection.

Shaving Mug, 3½" h, exhibits detailed applied floral work in white on a light green background. The name "C. W. Bowman" is written in white on an attached "card" held in place by the flowers; rare item.
$1,200.00–1,400.00.
Wetzel Collection.

Lotus Ware

Creamer and Sugar Sets
Cups and Saucers
Jewel Boxes
Match Holder
Perfume Ewers
Pin Tray
Photo Holder
Salt Cellars

Creamer, 3½" h, and Open Sugar, 2" h x 4" d, catalog #249, Chestnut design; the body of this set has small beads scattered over the exterior; gold sponged work accents the top borders and interior of the bowl.
$400.00–500.00 set.
Wetzel Collection.

Creamer and Sugar, Chestnut design, catalog #249, decorated with gold paste floral designs.
$450.00–550.00 set.
Wetzel Collection.

Coffee Cup, 2½" h x 3½" d, and Saucer 6" d, gold paste branches and leaves with pink dahlias; KT&K Mark 5.
$150.00–175.00.

Cup, 2" h, and Saucer, 5" d, after-dinner size; a salmon-pink glaze on the interior of the cup as well as at the base and in the center of the saucer with similarly colored flowers distinguish this set.
$125.00–150.00.
Wetzel Collection.

After-Dinner Cup, 2½" h,
and Saucer, 5" d, catalog #228,
Mecca design; light green geometric
designs outlined with gold stippled work.
$125.00–150.00.
Wetzel Collection.

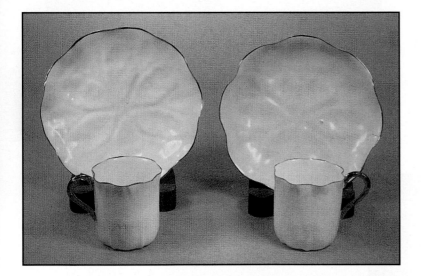

After-Dinner Cups, 1¾" h, and Saucers, catalog #256,
Oriental design; light pink glaze around outer borders
of saucers and cups with gold trim.
$175.00–200.00 each.
Wetzel Collection.

Tea Cup decorated with small
floral designs on interior.
$70.00–90.00.

Tea Cup, 1½" h x 4" d, and Saucer, 6¼" d,
Globe design, catalog #94; gold floral
design on light yellow background.
$125.00–150.00.
Wetzel Collection.

Tea Cup, 1½" h x 4" d, and Saucer, 6½" d, Globe
design, #94; gold paste clover decor with light
pink tint on interior of cup and light blue tint on
exterior; the saucer is decorated with a pink
center and a wide blue interior border.
$150.00–175.00.
Wetzel Collection.

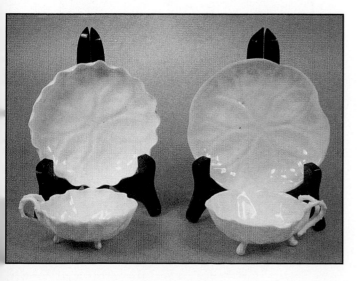

Tea Cups and Saucers, catalog #255, Sonoma design;
the body mold has a lightly sculpted leaf design, and
the cups have individual feet.
$125.00–150.00 each set.
Wetzel Collection.

Jewel Boxes: left, 4¾" h; right, 5½" h; catalog #262, described as "Jewel Box with filigree cover." The handles are also made with a filigree or open-work design. Turquoise, coral, and gold decorate the beaded designs. The box on the left has a matte cream colored finish. $1,000.00–1,200.00 each.
Wetzel Collection.

Match Holder, 4" l, open-work body design with beaded work on body and border; rare item. $700.00–900.00.
Wetzel Collection.

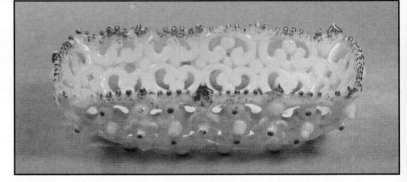

Perfume Ewer, 3½" h x 3" w, catalog #252, with twig shaped handle, undecorated. $700.00–800.00.
Wetzel Collection.

Perfume Ewer, 3½" h x 3" w, catalog #252; four feet with filigreed body, no handle, gold sponged work around neck and on feet. $500.00–600.00.
Wetzel Collection.

Fan Pin Tray, 6" 1, catalog #235;
semi-nude woman reclining with fan
behind her; hand-painted finish; rare item.
$1,200.00–1,500.00.
Wetzel Collection.

Photo Holders: left, 4" h x 5" w; Right, 4½" h x 5½" w;
catalog #254, described as "Coral Photo Holder"
because of the shape of the piece;
left, undecorated;
right, decorated with a coral finish.
Left, $300.00–400.00.
Right, $350.00–450.00.
Wetzel Collection.

Salt Cellars, ⅜" h x 1½" d, catalog #253,
described as "Individual Salts," gold
luster finish on interiors.
$70.00–90.00 each.
Wetzel Collection.

Lotus Ware

Jugs
Pitchers

Globe Jug, 5" h x 7" w, catalog #245;
large dark pink roses on body with a dark green
finish on handle and neck; gold enameled flowers
and gold trim accent neck and handle.
$700.00–800.00.
Wetzel Collection.

Globe Jug, 5" h x 7" w, catalog #245;
small pink flowers and stylized gold tulips
decorate body with turquoise bead work;
handle and neck are decorated with a
dark green finish with hand-painted gold
flowers and gold trim.
$700.00–800.00.
Wetzel Collection.

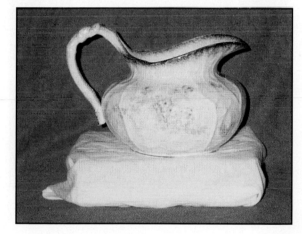

Leaf Jug, 5" h x 7" w, catalog #284; delicate pink
and green floral design with sponged gold trim.
$800.00–900.00.
Wetzel Collection.

Leaf Jug, 5" h x 7" w, catalog #284,
undecorated.
$600.00–700.00.
Wetzel Collection.

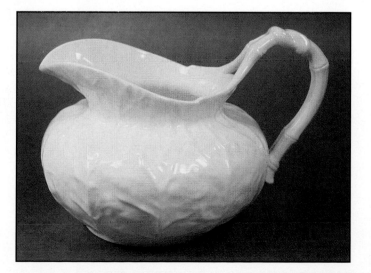

Valenciennes Jug, 3¼" h, catalog #247; hand-painted multicolored pansies on brown background are painted on panels alternating with gold fishnet work over a green finish, non-factory decoration.
$350.00–450.00.
Wetzel Collection.

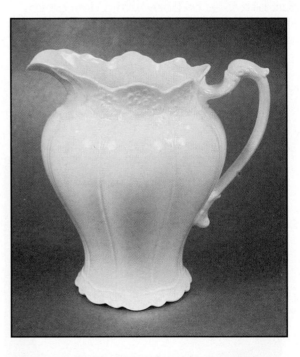

Pitcher, 7" h, light embossed floral designs around neck, scalloped base, undecorated.
$450.00–550.00.
Wetzel Collection.

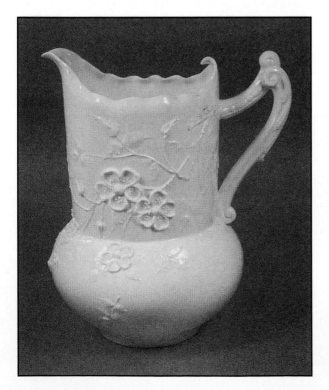

Pitcher, 9¼" h, applied floral slip work decorates body of this white ware piece; rare item.
$1,500.00–2,000.00.
Wetzel Collection.

Lotus Ware

Rose Bowls

Rose Jars

The Rose Bowls are called "Columbia Bowls" in the Knowles, Taylor & Knowles Lotus Ware catalog. Different numbers designate various types of applied decoration. (See Catalog Numbers 219–224 and 236–238 for Lotus Ware in the appendices.) The shape or mold of the bowls was either a rounded body with a crimped neck or an oblong body with a pinched, crimped neck. The Gipsy Kettles also have the same round body of the Columbia Bowls with the addition of vertical branch style handles. The name "Columbia" was used to commemorate the 400th year of the discovery of America by Columbus (Gates, 1992: 19). Another source suggests the name was given in recognition of the title of the 1893 Chicago's World Fair, the Columbian Exposition (Echoes, 1989).

Columbia Bowl, 4½" h; no specific catalog number is shown for this bowl which is decorated with applied flowers and leaves painted entirely in gold on a celadon body.
$1,200.00–1,500.00.
Wetzel Collection.

Columbia Bowl, 4" h x 5" w; applied floral decor painted lavender-blue with gold trim around the lightly ruffled neck; KT&K Mark 5.
$500.00–600.00.
Wetzel Collection.

Columbia Bowl, 4½" h, catalog #237; turquoise bead work on gold background on top two-thirds of body with hand-painted flowers on lower part of bowl, signed "E.T.D., 1898," non-factory decoration.
$600.00–700.00.
Wetzel Collection.

Columbia Bowl, 4½" h, catalog #237; pink roses on dark maroon background, signed "Xmas 96," non-factory decoration.
$500.00–600.00.
Wetzel Collection.

Columbia Bowl, 4½" h, catalog #222, applied flowers, leaves, and branches painted gold. $600.00–700.00.
Wetzel Collection.

Columbia Bowl, 4¾" h, catalog #238; lacy, applied open-work forms a built up design on the exterior of this bowl which is highlighted in gold. $800.00–1,000.00.
Wetzel Collection.

Columbia Bowl, 4¾" h, catalog #238; this example is the same as the preceding bowl, but it is unpainted. The intricate filigree pattern can be more easily seen.
$700.00–900.00.
Wetzel Collection.

Columbia Bowl, 4¼" h, applied chains and filigreed medallions on exterior of bowl. This piece is noted as having been a wedding gift from Bert Harker to Robert E. Boyce and Mary Louise Hallett in August, 1927. Robert Boyce was an officer of the Harker Pottery, another East Liverpool factory. $1,200.00–1,400.00.
Wetzel Collection.

Columbia Bowl, 4¾" h x 5⅜" 1, catalog #219; applied flowers and filigreed handles compose this design. The flowers are tinted pink matching the body finish around the handles, gold trim. $700.00–800.00.
Wetzel Collection.

Columbia Bowl, 4½" h x 5½" d, catalog #236; this design has the same filigreed handles as the preceding one, #219, but it does not have the applied floral work. The decoration consists of large hand-painted mauve mums, signed "M.I.W., 1894" on base, non-factory decoration. $700.00–800.00.
Wetzel Collection.

Columbia Bowl, 4" h x 6" d, 1½" opening at top, catalog #509. This bowl is an example of the Columbia bowl with a pinched neck. The pattern consists of large applied flowers and leaves with filigreed handles. The dark olive finish of the piece accentuates the white floral work; rare item; professionally repaired. $2,000.00–2,500.00.
Wetzel Collection.
Photograph furnished by Wiebold, Inc., Terrace Park, Ohio.

Columbia Bowl, 4⅝" h x 6¼" 1 with pinched neck. This bowl is the same shape as the preceding one and also has the same filigreed handles. It does not have applied floral work. Hand-painted violet colored flowers decorate the surface with handles and neck painted gold, non-factory decoration. $400.00–500.00.
Wetzel Collection.

Avignon Rose Jar, 6¾" h x 6½" w, catalog #240. The base has the same filigreed pattern as Columbia Bowl #238; undecorated. $1,400.00–1,600.00.
Wetzel Collection.

Orleans Rose Jar, 8½" h x 7" w, catalog #239. Although the body shape is the same as catalog #238, note the difference in the base and lid of this piece from the Avignon Rose Jar shown in the preceding picture. Gold and turquoise highlight some of the bead work on this piece. $1,500.00–1,700.00.
Wetzel Collection.

Persian Rose Jar, 8¼" h x 7" w, catalog #241. This design is distinguished by raised handles in addition to the filigreed medallions. The base and lid are like catalog #239. Light pink and violet flowers are painted in a random pattern on the body with gold highlighting the filigree and bead work. An interesting historical note about this piece is that it was owned by Lida Thompson, niece of coal baron, J. V. Thompson. She married Tharin Und Taxis, the Austrian prince. $1,800.00–2,000.00.
Wetzel Collection.

Gipsy Kettle, 7½" h; catalog #205 on the page for KT&K Belleek wares shows this piece without applied work. This bowl and the following one have applied floral and fish scale work. This example is undecorated. $800.00–1,000.00.
Wetzel Collection.

Gipsy Kettle, 7½" h; pink flowers and green leaves on lower body with gold fish scale work on upper border; KT&K Mark 5. $900.00–1,100.00.
Wetzel Collection.

Lotus Ware

Shell Trays

Shell Tray, catalog #201, 5¼" 1 x 5" w; decorated for the Pittsburgh Commandry; gold stenciled work and gold trim; KT&K Marks 5 and 6 (see photo below). $150.00–200.00.
Wetzel Collection.

Marks on preceding Shell Tray illustrating that the KT&K/China Mark was used on Lotus Ware. See photo above left.

Shell Tray, 5" h x 5½" w, catalog #201. All of the Shell Trays have the same catalog number. They came in four sizes. This example has hand-painted gold leaves with light enamel work, brushed gold trim. $200.00–250.00.

Shell Tray, 4" h x 4¼" w; hand-painted dogwood blossoms, gold trim, non-factory decoration. $200.00–250.00.
Wetzel Collection.

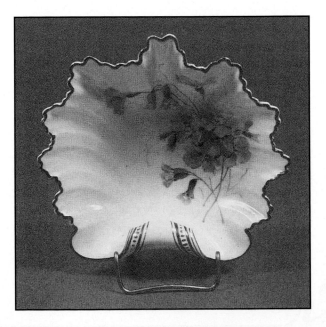

Shell Tray, 5" h x 5½" w; transfer figural decor of two girls in Victorian dress with one holding a basket of flowers; green finish on border, gold trim. $400.00–500.00.

Shell Tray, 5" h x 5½" w; transfer figural decor of two Victorian girls with one holding flowers and the other holding a lamb. The border finish and gold trim match the tray in the preceding photograph. $400.00–500.00.

Shell Tray, 7½" h x 8¾" w; transfer portrait of a Victorian woman with fancy bonnet; gold trim. $500.00–600.00.
Wetzel Collection.

Shell Tray, 5" h x 5½" w; transfer decor of two Cupids, gold trim. $300.00–400.00.

Shell Tray, 5½" h x 6" w; gold and turquoise enameled floral design on left side of tray, gold trim. $300.00–350.00.

Shell Tray, 5" h x 5½" w; hand-painted green pods and leaves near handle, gold trim. $300.00–350.00. *Wetzel Collection.*

Shell Tray, 7½" h x 8¾" w; tiny pink roses overlaid with enameled gold leaves and branches in center of dish, gold trim. $500.00–600.00. *Wetzel Collection.*

Shell Tray, 7½" h x 8¾" w; gold paste floral design on one side of tray against a pale cream background. $550.00–650.00.
Wetzel Collection.

Shell Tray, 5½" h x 6" w; pastel tulips with gold enameled leaves form an Art Nouveau pattern; gold trim. $450.00–500.00.
Wetzel Collection.

Shell Tray, 5" h x 5½" w; transfer design of pink roses in center of tray with a garland of yellow roses around inner border and single pink roses scattered around outer border. $300.00–400.00.
Crain Collection.

Lotus Ware

Flower Bowls

Jardinieres

Loving Cup

Flower bowl, 4½" h, three feet, catalog #214. This particular design has a narrow free-form opening at top with applied leaves and berries on the body. This undecorated example illustrates the detail of the workmanship.
$500.00–600.00.
Wetzel Collection.

Flower bowl, 4½" h, catalog #214; red berries with gold and bronze colored leaves.
$600.00–700.00.
Wetzel Collection.

Flower Bowl, 4½" h, catalog #214; gold leaves with thin red veining accented with shades of light blue on some leaves and berries; KT&K Mark 5.
$600.00–700.00.
Wetzel Collection.

Fern Jardiniere, 5" h x 14" d (handle to handle). The Lotus Ware catalog indicates that two sizes of Fern Jardinieres were made, an 8 inch and a 10 inch, catalog #271 and #278. This example is the same shape but the size is different. Rough textured branch style handles are decorated in gold with a hand-painted pastel floral design on the body, non-factory decoration.
$1,200.00–1,400.00.
Wetzel Collection.

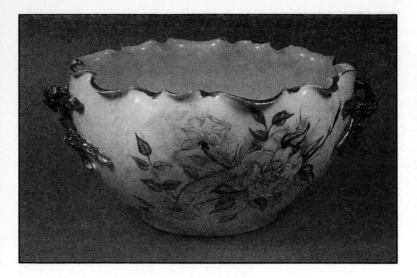

Fern Jardiniere, 5" h x 10" d, catalog #278; large hand-painted pink flowers on exterior with a pink finish on the interior, gold trim, non-factory decoration. $1,000.00–1,200.00.
Wetzel Collection.

Jardiniere, 14" d x 6½" h, Rustic design, #250; white ware with applied decor of shells and coral in the manner of some decoration found on Irish Belleek. $1,200.00–1,400.00.
Wetzel Collection.

Rustic Jardiniere, 5" h x 10" d, catalog #250. The applied work is quite heavy and rough textured combined with some light body sculpting which is visible on this undecorated example. $1,000.00–1,200.00.
Wetzel Collection.

Rustic Jardiniere, 7" h x 10½" d. This piece seems to be the same as catalog #251, but the size is not the same. The applied work has a light turquoise finish outlining a pink-beige leaf; gold trim, light blue-gray finish on body, non-factory decoration. $1,200.00–1,500.00.
Wetzel Collection.

Rustic Jardiniere, 6½" h x 13" d, the same as catalog #250, except for size; note the concave section in the center of the piece; textured designs painted gold with a coral finish on the interior.
$2,500.00–3,000.00.
Wetzel Collection.

Jardiniere, 7½" h x 6¾" d. This is a larger example of a Columbia Bowl shown in the preceding photographs under Rose Bowls. Elaborate chain designs and filigree medallions were applied to the body; rare item.
$1,400.00–1,800.00.
Wetzel Collection.

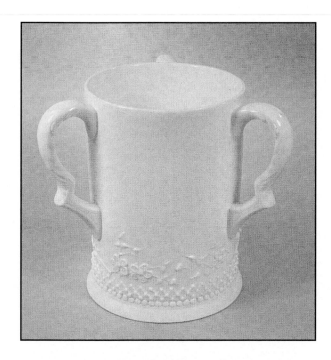

Loving Cup or Trophy Vase, 7" h, three handles; applied floral work and fishnet designs on base, undecorated.
$1,200.00–1,400.00.
Wetzel Collection.

Centerpiece, 5¾" h x 8¼" d. This pedestal bowl has four sections on the exterior to serve as bud vases. A transfer portrait of the semi-bare bust of a woman decorates the center.
$2,200.00–2,500.00.
Wetzel Collection.

Lotus Ware

Vases and Ewers

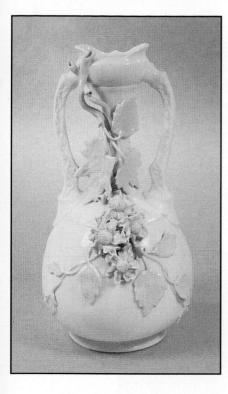

Arcanian Vase, 8½" h, catalog #504; applied flowers decorated with a celadon glaze on a white body. The Catalog indicates that this particular style of vase was made with white flowers on a celadon body or an olive body. $1,800.00–2,000.00.
Wetzel Collection.

Cremonian Vase, 6¼" h, catalog #285; hand-painted pink and white flowers with light enameling in white; green finish on neck, gold trim. $500.00–600.00.
Wetzel Collection.

Cremonian Vase, 6¼" h, catalog #507. This vase is the same shape as the preceding vase, but the catalog number is different because this version has applied floral work. This style of vase was available with white flowers on a celadon body like this example or with white flowers on an olive body. $1,000.00–1,200.00.
Wetzel Collection.

Egyptian Vase, 15" h, catalog #232. (The Egyptian vase is also shown as catalog #275 with filigree work consisting of chains and medallions.) This example is decorated with the figural portrait of a semi-nude woman with wings against a dark brown background, highlighted with golden-bronze enameled work and trim. $3,000.00–3,500.00.
Wetzel Collection.

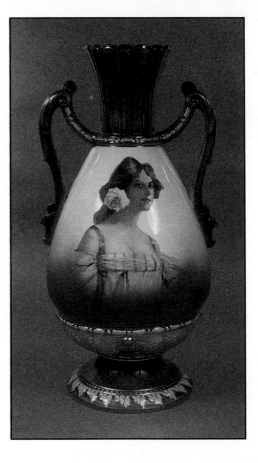

Egyptian Vase, 15" h, catalog #232; portraits of two Victorian women are featured, one on the front and one on the back, the work of Harry Thompson, a decorator at the factory. $3,000.00–3,500.00.
Wetzel Collection.

Egyptian Vase, reverse side of preceding piece.

62

Egyptian Vase, 15" h, catalog #232; gold paste leaves and enameled blue flowers decorate the body; the neck has tiny enameled white flowers on a dark blue background; the base has pâte sur pâte work in the Minton style; handles and trim have a heavy gold finish. This vase is from the Taylor family. $4,000.00–4,500.00.
Wetzel Collection.

Etruscan Vase, 10" h, catalog #270; white ware with filigreed handles and some applied floral and bead work on neck. $1,200.00–1,500.00.
Wetzel Collection.

Etruscan Vase, 10" h, catalog #272. This version of the vase is distinguished from #270 by a filigreed medallion at the top of the neck; hand-painted pink flowers with gold highlighting the filigreed work and handles; turquoise accents some of the bead work. $1,500.00–1,800.00.
Wetzel Collection.

Etruscan Vase, 10" h, catalog #272, filigreed work painted gold on a very dark matte green background. $1,800.00–2,000.00.
Wetzel Collection.

Etruscan Vase, 9" h, catalog #209; hand-painted yellow and red roses with green foliage on blue background highlighted by gold trim; artist initialed "MLK" on base. $1,000.00–1,200.00.
Wetzel Collection.

Etruscan Ewer, 10" h, catalog #230. This Etruscan style does not have filigree work; hand-painted figural decor of a reaper in a field framed with enameled gold scroll work; a dark coral finish overlaid with gold designs decorates the neck with a lighter coral finish on the interior of the neck; violets are painted on the reverse side (not shown). $1,000.00–1,200.00.
Wetzel Collection.

Etruscan Ewer, 10" h, catalog #248, heavy filigree work on base of ewer like that used on the Columbia bowl, catalog #240. Gold applied to some of the filigree and bead designs with blues, greens, and pinks painted between and on the filigree work which is not gold. $2,400.00–2,600.00.
Wetzel Collection.

Etruscan Ewer, 9½" h, catalog #503, applied white flowers, branches, and leaves on a celadon body. Another decoration for #503 was white applied work on an olive body. The Etruscan shape was also made in #209, a vase without filigree or bead work, a smooth body like ewer #230; #268, a ewer with applied floral designs; #274, a ewer with bead work on neck and top of bulbous base. $2,000.00–2,200.00.
Wetzel Collection.

Grecian Vase, 6" h, catalog #508; small pink and lavender flowers decorate the body, accented by green leaves; the neck exhibits pâte sur pâte work, in the Minton vein, on a blue background; KT&K Mark 5. $600.00–800.00.

Grecian Vases, 6¼" h, catalog #508; applied white flowers on an olive background. Each vase has a different floral design; this shape was also made with white flowers on a celadon body. $1,500.00–1,600.00 each.
Wetzel Collection.

Grecian Vase, 6" h, catalog #213; hand-painted multicolored birds perched on floral branches against white background on lower body; the upper body and neck have a light pink finish overlaid with floral designs outlined in gold. $400.00–600.00.
Wetzel Collection.

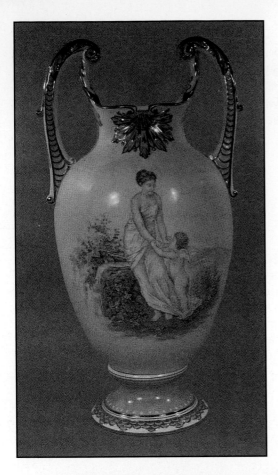

Ionian Vase, 18" h, catalog #233. The Ionian vase was also made with ornate filigree work and was noted as #281 in the catalog. A transfer design of a woman and a cherub holding hands; sepia tint, gold trim, light green finish on pedestal base. $2,500.00–3,000.00.
Wetzel Collection.

Ionian Vase, 18" h, catalog #233; hand-painted roses, dark green finish on handles and base, non-factory decoration. $1,800.00–2,000.00.
Wetzel Collection.

Laconian Vase, 13¼" h, catalog #257; base is bolted to the body. This version of the Laconian vase has large and small filigreed medallions and beaded chain work. Another style, catalog #264, does not have the applied design. On this vase, the beading has been painted as jewels with turquoise, coral, and gold. $6,000.00–6,500.00.
Wetzel Collection.

Lily Vase, 8" h, #98 on the catalog page for Belleek wares and #211 for the page showing Lotus Ware; blue, pink, and cream colored finishes decorate exterior of vase, gold trim; KT&K Mark 5.
$1,000.00–1,200.00.
Wetzel Collection.

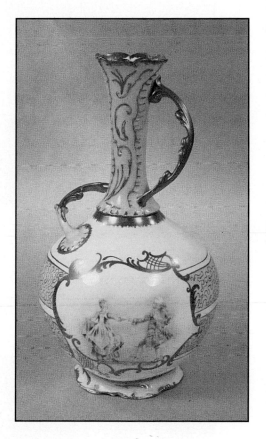

Parmian Vase, 10" h, catalog #286; hand-painted couple in colonial dress, dancing; light green background, gold trim.
$1,000.00–1,200.00.
Wetzel Collection.

Parmian Vase, 10" h, catalog #286; transfer decor of pink roses on light green shading to dark green background, gold trim.
$1,000.00–1,100.00.
Wetzel Collection.

Parmian Vase, 10" h, catalog #500; applied white flowers on celadon body glaze. $2,200.00–2,400.00.
Wetzel Collection.

Parmian Vases, 10" h, catalog #500; applied white flowers on olive body glaze. The Parmian Vases, #286 and #500 feature an Art Nouveau style handle in a curving design around the neck. $2,200.00–2,400.00 each.
Wetzel Collection.

Roman Vase, 10" h, catalog #210; white ware. $800.00–1,000.00.

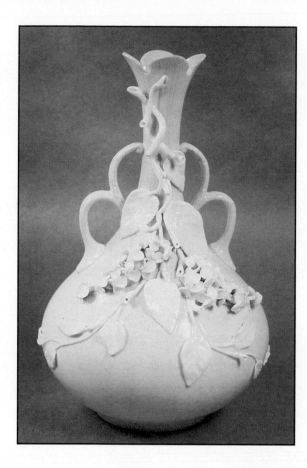

Roman Vase, 10" h, catalog #510; this is the same as #210 except the body has been decorated with applied floral and leaf designs, white on celadon.
$2,200.00–2,400.00.
Wetzel Collection.

Roman Vase, 10" h, catalog #510; white applied floral pattern on an olive body.
$2,200.00–2,400.00.
Wetzel Collection.

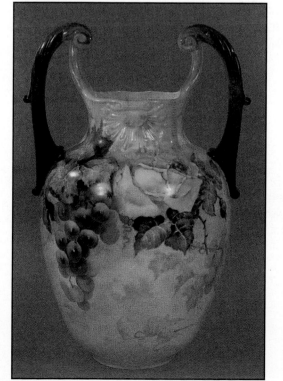

Savonian Vase, 15" h, catalog #234. This vase is the same as Ionian #233 except it does not have the pedestal base; hand-painted roses and grapes, dark green finish on handles, non-factory decoration.
$2,400.00–2,800.00.
Wetzel Collection.

Savonian Vase, 15" h; hand-painted seated woman in long gown with a Cupid perched on her back; light cream-colored background, gold trim, non-factory decoration. $2,400.00–2,800.00.
Wetzel Collection.

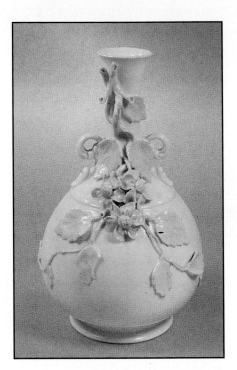

Syrian Vase, 8" h, catalog #505; applied floral work with a celadon finish on white body. This mold was also made as catalog #289 without any applied work. $2,000.00–2,200.00.
Wetzel Collection.

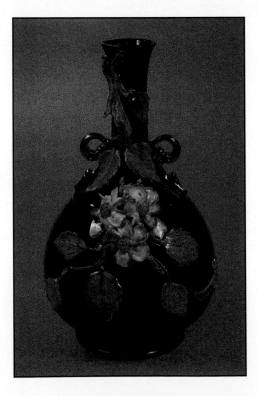

Syrian Vase, 8" h, catalog #505; applied floral designs in white with tinted pink edges; leaves and stems finished with a light green color contrasting sharply to the olive finish on the body; gold outlining on the leaves and gold handles. The catalog describes this vase with white flowers on an olive body, but it does not include this fancier version. $2,200.00–2,400.00.
Wetzel Collection.

Syrian Vase, 8" h, catalog #283. Fishnet designs around the upper body differentiate this example from #505; undecorated.
$800.00–1,000.00.
Russo Collection.

Thebian Vase, 9" h, catalog #287; hand-painted woman with two children in garden, gold trim, non-factory decoration.
$1,000.00–1,200.00.
Wetzel Collection.

Thebian Vase, 9" h, catalog #287; hand-painted white flowers with light pink edges and yellow centers, gold scroll designs on body.
$800.00–1,000.00.
Wetzel Collection.

Thebian Vases, 9" h, catalog #501, applied white flowers on celadon body.
$2,000.00–2,200.00 each.
Wetzel Collection.

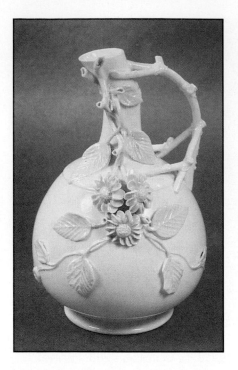

Thebian Vase, 9" h, catalog #501; applied white flowers on olive body. $2,000.00–2,200.00. *Wetzel Collection.*

Tiberian Ewer, 7" h, catalog #506; applied flowers and leaves with a celadon glaze on a white body; this ewer was also made with white flowers on an olive body. $2,000.00–2,200.00. *Wetzel Collection.*

Tiberian Ewer, 7", catalog #282. This and the following four photographs illustrate the Tiberian ewer without applied decoration. The rough textured branch style handle distinguishes the Tiberian design. Transfer pattern of small pink daisies on body with sponged gold work on handle. $1,000.00–1,200.00. *Wetzel Collection.*

Tiberian Ewer, 7" h, Catalog #282; hand-painted pink flowers with green leaves, gold accents on handle and neck, non-factory decoration. This example of catalog #282 has a variation to the mold with four indentations on the four sides of the body. One of those is visible in the photograph. This type of "dimpling" is found also on some other examples of Lotus ware. *Wetzel Collection.* $1,000.00–1,200.00.

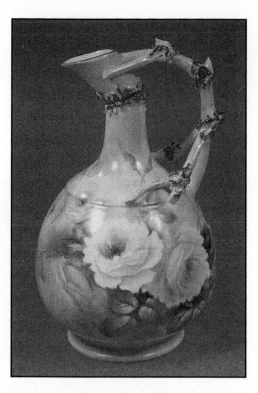

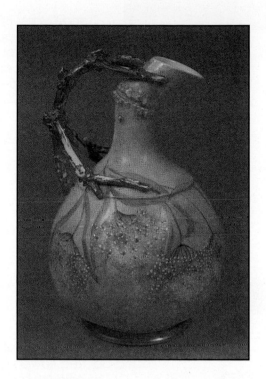

Tiberian Ewer, 7" h, catalog #282; large hand-painted pink, white, and red roses on pale blue background; gold highlights rough textured work on handle and neck, non-factory decoration.
$1,000.00–1,200.00.
Wetzel Collection.

Tiberian Ewer, 7" h, catalog #282, hand-painted pale green flowers overlaid with small white enameled flowers with yellow centers; body shades from light cream to light coral, gold trim, non-factory decoration.
$1,000.00–1,200.00.
Wetzel Collection.

Tiberian Ewer, 7" h, catalog #282; hand-painted pastel floral designs outlined with gold enameling on a pale green matte background, gold paste and white enameling accent floral centers; the exterior of the spout has a highly glazed light pink finish; heavily sponged gold applied to handle and neck.
$1,600.00–1,800.00.
Dunajeski Collection.

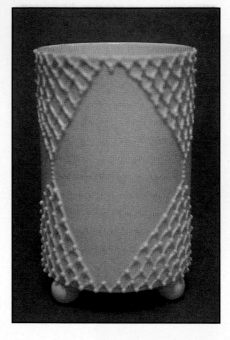

Tuscan Vase, 8" h, catalog #276; fishnet designs form diamond shaped panels on vase; the Tuscan vase has a round can or cylinder shape, and it was made with several other applied decorations of a fishnet or floral type (catalog #215–#218 and #277 and #280); undecorated. $500.00–600.00.

Tuscan Vase, 8" h, catalog #216; three panels of hand-painted flowers alternate with three panels of gold fishnet work; artist initialed "JWO." $600.00–800.00.
Wetzel Collection.

Tuscan Vase, 8" h, catalog #218; fish scale work around border of neck and applied bell shaped flowers with long, slender leaves; the floral designs are painted with a lavender Chelsea Grape luster-type finish accented with gold stems. $800.00–1,000.00.
Wetzel Collection.

Tuscan Vase, 8" h, catalog #217; the applied floral and leaf work on body has been decorated with gold painted leaves and enameled flowers with a mauve luster; signed "E. M. S. 96" on base, non-factory decoration. $1,000.00–1,200.00.
Wetzel Collection.

Tuscan Vase, 8½" h, catalog #242. There is no description given for catalog #242, but the body of the vase and feet appear to be the same as the Tuscan models. Very ornate filigreed designs applied on lower half of vase with large beads around top border and applied small flowers at points around top half of vase.
$1,500.00–1,800.00.
Wetzel Collection.

Tuscan Vase, 8½" h, catalog #242; hand-painted lavender flowers with green leaves have been added to the vase with gold highlighting some of the filigree work, matte finish, non-factory decoration.
$1,800.00–2,000.00.
Wetzel Collection.

Tuscan Vase, 8½" h, catalog #242; the bisque body of this example was not glazed. All pieces of Lotus Ware had this matte appearance before the glaze was applied to them and then refired.
$400.00–500.00.
Wetzel Collection.

Umbrian Vase, 9" h; applied celadon flowers on a white body. This decoration is not listed in the catalog, but #502 is shown for the Umbrian vase with either white flowers on a celadon or olive body; the Umbrian vase without applied decoration is listed as #288. $2,000.00–2,200.00.
Wetzel Collection.

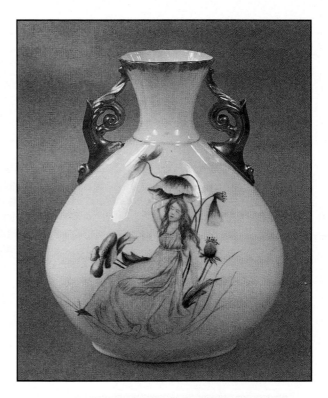

Umbrian Vase, 8½" h, catalog #288; hand-painted girl in long yellow dress surrounded by large pink poppies; gold trim.
$1,200.00–1,400.00.
Wetzel Collection.

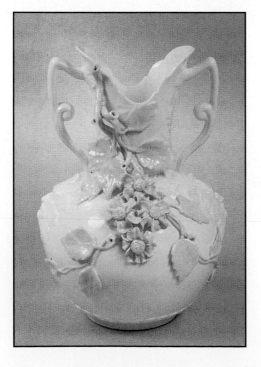

Venetian Vase, 8½" h, catalog #511; applied flowers in celadon on white body. This shape was also made with white flowers on a celadon or olive body. It is also listed as catalog #212 without applied floral work.
$2,000.00–2,200.00.
Wetzel Collection.

Semi-Vitreous Wares

Commemorative and Decorative China

William McKinley Souvenir Plate, circa 1894. McKinley was governor of Ohio before he was elected President of the United States in 1897. He was a friend of John N. Taylor and often visited with him in East Liverpool. Taylor was a member of the governor's staff for four years (McCord, 1905: 832, 383).
$150.00–200.00.
Collection of the East Liverpool Museum of Ceramics.

Plate, 8" d, transfer decor of couple in medieval dress, KT&K Mark 8 with a Masonic emblem and "Riddle Lodge, East Liverpool, Ohio."
$85.00–110.00.
Wetzel Collection.

Plate 8" d, Romeo and Juliet transfer with border matching plate in preceding photograph and marked the same.
$85.00–110.00.
Wetzel Collection.

Plate, 8" d, game birds with a wide dark blue border over-laid with gold stenciled designs; "Pittsburgh Commandery" is printed at the top of the plate; "No. 1 K. T." in the middle (on either side of the birds); "1898 Twenty Seventh Trien-niel" is printed at the bottom of the plate; KT&K Mark 8.
$65.00–75.00.
Wetzel Collection.

Plate, 8" d, cherubs in center with "Pittsburgh Commandery" printed at the top; "No. 1 K. T." in the middle; and "1900 State Conclave Wilkes-Barre, PA" at the bottom. The wide wine border with gold stenciled designs matches the preceding plate; KT&K Mark 8.
$75.00–85.00.
Wetzel Collection.

Plate, 8½" d, commemorating the Pittsburgh Commandery 28th Triennial in Louisville, Kentucky, in 1901; transfer portrait of man in ceremonial dress, entitled "Marechal Léfebuxe" at base of portrait; cobalt blue border; KT&K Mark 7.
$100.00–125.00.
Wetzel Collection.

Plate, 8½" d, commemorating the Pittsburgh Commandery 28th Triennial in Louisville, Kentucky, in 1901; transfer portrait of bust of woman in pink gown, entitled "Madame Sans-Géne" at base of portrait; cobalt blue border matching preceding plate; KT&K Mark 7.
$100.00–125.00.
Wetzel Collection.

Plate, 8" d, transfer scene depicting the Crusades; iridescent wine border; made for the Pittsburgh Commandery 29th Triennial in San Francisco, California, in 1904; KT&K Mark 7; the original box (not shown) for this plate was still intact. The presentation box indicates that these types of commemorative plates were special items intended to be souvenirs and preserved.
$100.00–125.00.
Wetzel Collection.

Plate, 8" d, transfer portrait of Victorian woman with long blonde hair; wide wine border with gold stenciled designs; made for the Pittsburgh Commandry, 29th Triennial, San Francisco, Cal., in 1904; KT&K Mark 7.
$100.00–125.00.
Mullins and Beck Collection.

Back of plate in preceding photograph.

Plate, 8" d, transfer figural decor of cowboy and cattle in center; Masonic and Commandery emblems on inner border with gold trim; made for the 1906 Toledo Commandery Annual Conclave; KT&K Mark 7 (entire mark).
$100.00–125.00.
Crain Collection.

Plate, 8¼" d, transfer scene entitled "Prodigal Returns"; gold luster border; made for the 1907 Pittsburgh Commandery 30th Triennial in Saratoga, New York; KT&K Mark 7.
$100.00–115.00.
Wetzel Collection.

Plate, 8¼" d, "Madame LeBrun and her Daughter" transfer decorates center with gold luster border; this plate was also a 1907 commemorative for the Pittsburgh Commandery; KT&K Mark 7.
$100.00–115.00.
Wetzel Collection.

Plate, 8" d, "Joan of Arc" transfer; wide gold border with elaborate stenciled designs; made for the 1907 Pittsburgh Commandery 30th Triennial in Saratoga, New York; KT&K Mark 7. $100.00–115.00.
Wetzel Collection.

Plate, 8" d, figural transfer of a shepherd and his flock with gold border matching preceding plate; it is also marked the same for the 1907 Pittsburgh Commandery 30th Triennial; KT&K Mark 7. $100.00–115.00.
Wetzel Collection.

Plate, 8" d, "Columbus Received on his Return" transfer scene, green border with gold stenciled designs; made for the 1910 Pittsburgh Commandery Triennial in Chicago; KT&K Mark 7. $60.00–75.00.
Wetzel Collection.

Plate, 8" d, portrait of woman with golden-red hair; border matches plate in preceding picture; made for the 1910 Pittsburgh Commandery Triennial in Chicago; KT&K Mark 7. $60.00–75.00.
Wetzel Collection.

Souvenir Plate for the Knights Templar in 1913 honoring the Grand Master, John P. L. Gobin 1889–1892. $60.00–75.00.
Collection of the East Liverpool Museum of Ceramics.

Commemorative Plate with transfer work inscribed "Arrival before Jerusalem"; marked Semi-Viterous Porcelain, circa 1890–1920. $65.00–75.00.
Collection of the East Liverpool Museum of Ceramics.

Plate, 9½" d, transfer decor of large yellow roses with "Guyeau" printed at base of design; gold border with Greek key design; KT&K Mark 9 with "Ramona" (as pattern name). $65.00–85.00.
Wetzel Collection.

Plate, 10" d, scenic transfer design featuring a long bridge and river with two figures in the foreground; wide cobalt blue border; KT&K Mark 8. $50.00–70.00.
Wetzel Collection.

Vase, 11" h, reclining tiger portrayed with a Flow Blue finish, KT&K Mark 9. $400.00–500.00.
Riecker Collection.

Vase, 11¼" h, transfer floral decoration of a white rose in the center of dark pink roses; KT&K Mark 9.
$120.00–140.00.
Wetzel Collection.

Vase, 14" h, hand-painted scene of a large body of water and mountains with forest and deer in the foreground, signed by factory artist Alf Potter; the mold maker was A. Geisz, signed and dated March 1922. This mold is the same as catalog #232, Egyptian, without the handles and pedestal base; KT&K Mark 9.
$1,200.00–1,400.00.
Wetzel Collection.

Vase, 14" h, hand-painted landscape with water and mountains similar to scenes in the preceding two pictures; signed by Alf Potter, 1921, unmarked.
$1,200.00–1,400.00.
Wetzel Collection.

Vase, 14" h, hand-painted mountain and lake scene by Alf Potter on same mold as above; KT&K Mark 9.
$1,200.00–1,400.00.
Wetzel Collection.

Lamp Base, 13" h; seasonal scenes are featured on four alternating panels of the piece; hand painted and signed by Alf Potter, 1923; unmarked.
$1,800.00–2,000.00.
Wetzel Collection.

(All four panels shown on this page.)

Fall foliage and a river are shown in this panel.

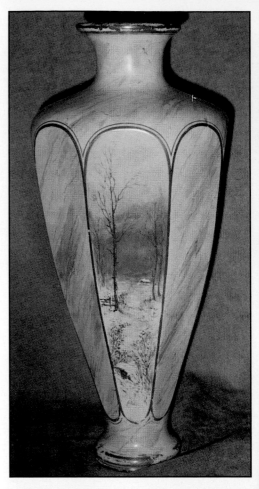

Winter scene with snow-covered ground and bare trees.

The foliage is green in this scene with long steps leading to a cottage.

Winding river in a green forest, perhaps a summer scene.

Salver, 15" d; hand-painted dogs in center with other creatures of nature painted in panels around the border; artist signed by Alf Potter, 1918; unmarked.
$1,200.00–1,400.00.
Wetzel Collection.

Alf Potter's signature and date on back of salver.

Chocolate Set: Pot, 8¾" h; 5 Cups, 3¼" h, and Saucers; hand-painted woods, water, and mountains, gold trim. The artwork on this set is by Alf Potter, although pieces are unsigned; KT&K Mark 9.
$800.00–1,000.00.
Wetzel Collection.

Chocolate Cup from set with
hand-painted river scene like the one
on the fourth panel of the lamp.
$150.00–200.00.

Chocolate Cup with hand-painted
waterfall. $150.00–200.00.

Chocolate Cup with hand-painted
evergreens and mountains.
$150.00–200.00.

Chocolate Cup with hand-painted winter
scene like the second panel on the lamp.
$150.00–200.00.

Chocolate Cup with hand-painted seascape
with sea gulls in the background.
$150.00–200.00.

Semi-Vitreous Wares

Wash Sets and Accessories

Wash Set, KT&K Mark 9; Bowl and Pitcher, gold stenciled flowers in a simple design with gold band trim; the following four photographs include the other pieces for this set. $800.00–1,000.00 set.
Ryan Collection.

Waste Jar.

Hot Water Pitcher.

Chamber Pot.

Shaving Mug.

View of complete set with the Soap Dish and
Toothbrush Holder shown in the middle foreground.

Pieces from a Wash Set, KT&K Mark 9; blue-green
finish on body with very dark green glaze on
deep borders; outlines of gold leaves and gold
sponged work accent borders; Chamber Pot,
5½" h x 8½" d.
$150.00–200.00.
Wetzel Collection.

Toothbrush Holder, 4" h. $75.00–100.00.

Pitcher, 11" h. $100.00–125.00.

Shaving Mug, 3½" h. $100.00–120.00.

Bowl, 16" d and Pitcher, 12" h, KT&K Mark 9; pink
and white floral transfer design on white body;
gold highlights the scroll work of the mold.
$250.00–300.00 set.
Wetzel Collection.

Pitcher, 8" h. $100.00–125.00.

Toothbrush Holder, 5" h. $50.00–75.00.

Shaving Mug, 4" h. $75.00–100.00.

Bowl, 16½" d and Pitcher, 12" h, KT&K Mark 9; transfer floral decor in a soft gray-blue color on white body.
$200.00–300.00 set.
Estell Collection.

Chamber Pot, 5" h, 10" d, with Lid and Shaving Mug, 4" h, matching preceding Bowl and Pitcher.
Chamber Pot, $75.00–100.00.
Shaving Mug, $50.00–60.00.

Waste Jar decorated with a transfer outline of flowers in a light blue; the neck is scalloped and floral designs are outlined on the upper part of the body; KT&K Semi-Vitreous Ware, circa 1900.
$175.00–225.00.
Collection of the
East Liverpool Museum of Ceramics.

Shaving Mug with a Flow Blue type floral design, circa 1890–1929.
$75.00–100.00.
Collection of the
East Liverpool Museum of Ceramics.

Small Pitcher (top),
Toothbrush Holder (middle), and
Shaving Mug (bottom) matching
preceding Bowl and Pitcher.
Pitcher, $100.00–125.00.
Toothbrush Holder, $50.00–75.00.
Shaving Mug, $75.00–100.00.

Pieces from a Wash Set displayed at the East
Liverpool Museum of Ceramics; gold flowers,
leaves, and vines on white body, circa 1890s.
Bowl and Pitcher Set, $300.00–400.00.
Covered Soap Dish, $70.00–90.00.

Bathroom Vanity, KT&K white ware,
circa 1895. These were designed to
hang on the wall and hold soap,
shaving brush, combs, and so forth.
$250.00–300.00.
Collection of the
East Liverpool Museum of Ceramics.

Bathroom Vanity made in the same design as the
preceding one; this example has transfer portraits on
the middle pockets and pink flowers decorate the
exterior of the base and top, gold trim.
$300.00–400.00.
Collection of the East Liverpool Museum of Ceramics.

Wash Set from the last quarter of the nineteenth century; green, brown, and yellow
flowers on a pale blue background with a darker blue border, gold trim.
Chamber Pot, $150.00–200.00 .
Shaving Mug, $75.00–100.00.
Covered Soap Dish, $75.00–100.00.
Pitcher, $100.00–120.00.
Collection of the East Liverpool Museum of Ceramics.

Bowl and Pitcher, Toothbrush Holder, and Covered Waste
Jar matching the pieces in the preceding picture.
Bowl and Pitcher Set, $300.00–350.00.
Covered Waste Jar, $300.00–400.00.
Toothbrush Holder, $50.00–75.00.

Chamber Pot, 5" h, 8¾" d, KT&K Mark 5; small enameled
gold flowers and leaves on yellow-cream colored background; a pitcher at the East Liverpool Museum of
Ceramics is decorated in the same manner with the art
work attributed to George Morley.
$200.00–250.00.
Wetzel Collection.

Pitcher, decorated by George Morley in 1894; gold paste enameled flowers on yellow-cream background; KT&K Mark 9. $300.00–350.00.
Collection of the East Liverpool Museum of Ceramics.

Shaving Mug, 3½" h, white ware; light embossed design around upper body, pleated neck design; KT&K Mark 5.
$50.00–75.00.
Wetzel Collection.

Covered Waste Jar with iris and bird hand-painted decoration, gold trim, circa 1900.
$300.00–400.00.
Collection of the East Liverpool Museum of Ceramics.

Shaving Mug, 3½" h, KT&K Mark 9; pink and white flowers, gold trim.
$60.00–85.00.
Wetzel Collection.

Pitchers from a Wash Set: 8" h and 12" h, large dark pink roses, gold trim, KT&K Mark 9.
Pitcher, 8" h, $70.00–80.00.
Pitcher, 12" h, $100.00–125.00.
Estell Collection.

Pitcher, 11" h, KT&K Mark 9; small pink and white flowers scattered over body, gold trim. $100.00–125.00.
Estell Collection.

Pitcher, 10¾" h, KT&K Mark 9; tiny pink rose garlands around base of neck with gold stenciled floral work around upper body, gold trim. $75.00–110.00.
Estell Collection.

Pitcher, 8" h, KT&K Mark 9; gold scroll work in an Art Nouveau style on a cream-colored background. $100.00–125.00.

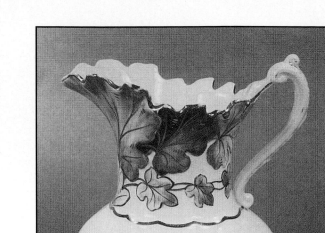

Pitcher, 8" h, KT&K Mark 9; hand-painted pink and green leaves outlined and veined in gold decorate the top half of the pitcher. $120.00–140.00.

Spittoon, 5¼" h, 8" d, KT&K Mark 10; simple gold band decoration. $140.00–160.00.
Wetzel Collection.

Princeton Spittoon, listed as #105 in the KT&K Hotel China catalog, 4½" h x 8½" d; large blue flowers on white body; KT&K Mark 10. $150.00–175.00.
Wetzel Collection.

Semi-Vitreous Wares

Hotel and Table China

Sauce boat, 5½" h x 9" w, KT&K Mark 11; undecorated. $35.00–45.00.
Wetzel Collection.

Sugar Bowl, 3½" h x 4½" d, KT&K Mark 10 with numbers "4 27 4" indicating 1927; this example is similar to #110 "Open Round Sugar, Thick" in the Hotel China catalog. This one has a rolled rim, however. Molded faces serve as handles; undecorated. $15.00–20.00.
Wetzel Collection.

Sugar Bowl, 3½" h x 3½" d, unmarked; the handles are the same molded faces as in the preceding example; undecorated. $15.00–20.00.
Wetzel Collection.

Oval Vegetable bowl 10½" 1, KT&K Mark 10 with the letters. "S.E.K." indicating the year 1925; undecorated. $12.00–15.00.
Wetzel Collection.

Dinner Plate, circa 1890–1929, undecorated. The scalloped border pattern is the same as the popular French Haviland "Ranson" pattern.
$15.00–20.00.
Collection of the East Liverpool Museum of Ceramics.

Dinner Plate, circa 1900–1929, transfer floral
pattern of a peacock and flowers.
$18.00–22.00.
Collection of the East Liverpool Museum of Ceramics.

Dinner Plate, circa 1900–1929; pattern around
outer border is composed of small pink roses
on a black background alternating with
double shield designs in gold.
$16.00–20.00.
Collection of the East Liverpool Museum of Ceramics.

Soup Bowl, circa 1925; suits of cards in black
and red form a border pattern.
$15.00–20.00.
Collection of the East Liverpool Museum of Ceramics.

Dinner Plate, circa 1890–1920; transfer pattern of
large coral colored flowers in an Oriental motif.
$20.00–25.00.
Collection of the East Liverpool Museum of Ceramics.

Dinner Plate, circa 1890–1929; a transfer blue floral scroll pattern decorates border with a center floral medallion; this particular pattern is identified as "No. 9" in the Hotel China catalog; it was also available in gray.
$18.00–22.00.
Collection of the East Liverpool Museum of Ceramics.

Dinner Plate, circa 1890–1929; repetitive design of clusters of small multicolored flowers with a large pink rose around the border.
$18.00–22.00.
Collection of the East Liverpool Museum of Ceramics.

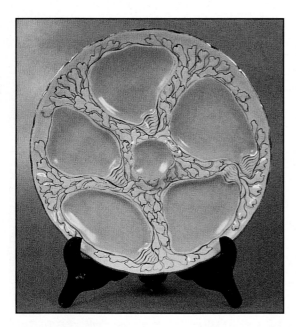

Oyster Plate, 8¾" d, KT&K Mark 10; a pink glaze decorates the sections of the plate in an open shell design with fancy gold outline work on the border and between the sections.
$40.00–50.00.

Dinner Service, KT&K Mark 11a. The following photographs show various pieces of the set; small pink roses framed by blue scroll work form a pattern around the border on a light cream-colored background; these are separated by thin gold lines connected by three tiny pink roses; the centers of the pieces are white; heavy gold trim.
Dinner Plate, 9" d; Salad Plate, 7¼" d; Bread & Butter Plate, 6¼" d.
Dinner Plate, $18.00–20.00.
Salad Plate, $10.00–12.00.
Bread & Butter Plate, $8.00–10.00.
Wetzel Collection.

Large Soup Bowl, 7¼" d; Fruit Bowl, 5¼" d;
Cup and Saucer.
Cup and Saucer, $15.00–18.00.
Soup Bowl, $12.00–15.00.
Fruit Bowl, $6.00–8.00.

Covered Sugar Bowl and Creamer.
$40.00–50.00 set.

Gravy Boat with Underplate. $25.00–35.00 set.

Round Covered Vegetable Dish, 10¼" d.
$35.00–45.00.

Oval Covered Vegetable Dish, 11½" 1. This set also
included an Oval Open Vegetable Dish, 7½" d; a Plat-
ter, 14½" 1; an Open Sauce Dish, 2½" h x 5¼" d; and a
Relish Dish, 9" 1.
Oval Covered Vegetable, $45.00–55.00.
Oval Open Vegetable (not shown), $25.00–35.00.
Platter (not shown), $30.00–40.00.
Open Sauce Dish (not shown), $8.00–10.00.
Relish Dish (not shown), $10.00–12.00.

Bread and Butter Plate, 6¾" d; KT&K Mark 10 with the year indicated by the numbers "27"; an abstract geometric design forms border pattern with clusters of small pink roses spaced around inner border.
$8.00–10.00.
Crain Collection.

Oval Covered Vegetable Bowl, KT&K Mark 6; small pink roses in reserves around border; gold trim.
$35.00–45.00.
Barney Collection.

Globe Molasses Can, #100 in the Hotel China catalog, metal collar and lid.
$175.00–225.00.
Collection of the East Liverpool Museum of Ceramics.

Syrup Pitcher or Molasses Jug, 4" h, hinged metal lid and metal collar; light pink finish on body with a satin glaze; KT&K Mark 5.
$200.00–250.00.
Wetzel Collection.

Leaf Jug, 5¼" h x 7" d; this is the same mold as
#285 in the Lotus Ware catalog; KT&K Mark 9;
light blue-green finish on body, gold trim.
$75.00–100.00.
Wetzel Collection.

Pitcher, circa 1890–1927; hand-painted
blue leaf pattern covers body with
undecorated handle.
$100.00–125.00.
Collection of the East Liverpool Museum of Ceramics.

Pitcher, 7¾" h, KT&K Mark 9; transfer decor of pink roses
on a light green shading to dark green body.
$140.00–160.00.
Wetzel Collection.

Rocaille Ice Jug, 9" h, #16 in the Hotel China catalog,
KT&K Mark 10; "Ice Water" stenciled in gold
with dark blue finish around neck.
$75.00–125.00.
Estell Collection.

Individual Coffee Pot, 5½" h, KT&K Mark 10 with letters "PIH" indicating the year 1922; clusters of muticolored flowers with one large pink rose form border pattern. This is the same pattern as previously shown on a dinner plate.
$60.00–75.00.
Wetzel Collection.

Mug, 6" h, KT&K Mark 9; green and red grapes on cream shading to dark brown body; ornately scalloped handle.
$100.00–125.00.
Wetzel Collection.

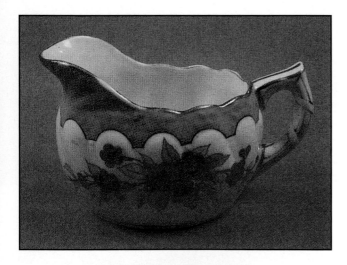

Creamer, 3" h x 4¼" 1, KT&K Mark 5; gold enameled flowers with multicolored leaves on body with dark blue finish on neck, gold trim.
$20.00–25.00.
Wetzel Collection.

Pitcher, 5¼" h, KT&K Mark 5; transfer floral designs of different varieties decorate the swirled panels of the body with an olive-green finish on neck and handle with gold highlights.
$30.00–35.00.
Wetzel Collection.

Pitcher, 7" h, KT&K Mark 5; this pitcher is decorated similarly to the preceding one, except the flowers are smaller and different, and the handle is undecorated.
$35.00–40.00.
Estell Collection.

Pitcher, circa 1890–1929; decal decoration of dancing figures and ducks in brown on white background.
$120.00–140.00.
Collection of the East Liverpool Museum of Ceramics.

Punch Bowl, 9½" h x 15½" d, KT&K Mark 10; "Tom & Jerry" (a type of popular punch) stenciled in gold on the body; blue finish on top border and pedestal base; autumn-colored flowers and leaves on interior, gold trim.
$350.00–450.00.
Estell Collection.

Footed Match Stand, 4½" h #117 in the Hotel China catalog; ribbed for striking a match; KT&K Mark 5, undecorated.
$50.00–60.00.
Wetzel Collection.

107

Match Holder, 2¾" h, KT&K Mark 5, light green finish with gold trim.
$40.00–50.00.
Wetzel Collection.

Match Holder similar to the preceding one but decorated with a cobalt blue border at top and bottom and in small designs on body.
$65.00–75.00.
Collection of The East Liverpool Museum of Ceramics.

Salesman's Sample of a Covered Vegetable Dish, 2" h x 5" w, unmarked on base but company name is printed on body.
$100.00–125.00.
Wetzel Collection.

Inkwell, 3" h x 6¼" l, made in the form of a Covered Vegetable Dish; KT&K Mark 10 with the letters "P.F.J." indicating the year 1924.
$75.00–100.00.
Wetzel Collection.

Child's Tea Set, KT&K Mark 5; an autumn leaf design forms a pattern on the body, gold trim. A similar "Little Gem" set is shown in the Appendices. The set includes: Plates, 4½" d; Cups, 2⅛" h x 2¼" d; Teapot, 5" h; Waste Bowl, 2⅛"hx3⅛"d; Covered Sugar Bowl, 4¼" h; Creamer, 3¼" h. The set is for six.
$400.00–500.00 set.
Wetzel Collection.

Whiskey Jugs

K. T. & K. Mark 5

Commercial Logos

Decorative Designs

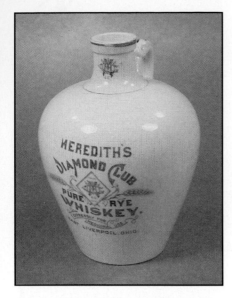

Meredith's Diamond Club Pure
Rye Whiskey, 5¼" h, half pint;
"Expressly for Medicinal Use"
printed on body.
$200.00–250.00.
Wetzel Collection.

Meredith's half pint with
original cork with
Meredith label on it.
$250.00–300.00.
Wetzel Collection.

Meredith's Diamond Club
Whiskey, 6" h, pint size which is
scarcer than other sizes.
$275.00–325.00.
Wetzel Collection.

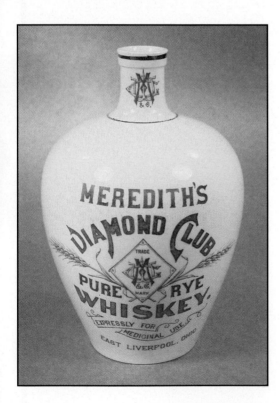

Meredith's Diamond Club Whiskey, Pure Rye, 6" h, pint.
$275.00–325.00.
Wetzel Collection.

Meredith's Diamond Club Pure Rye Whiskey, 8¼" h, quart. This and
the following two examples are the same except for some variation
on the printed logos. This one includes "East Liverpool, Ohio," and
has the Meredith monogram printed on the upper body.
$150.00–200.00.
Wetzel Collection.

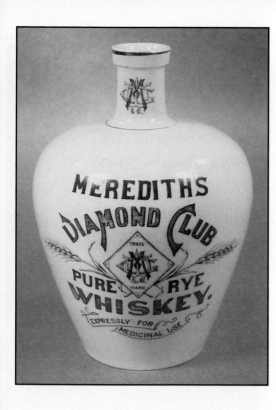

This Jug has the Meredith monogram printed on the neck and does not have "East Liverpool, Ohio" printed on the body. $150.00–200.00.
Wetzel Collection.

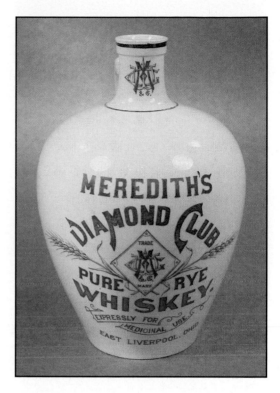

This example has "East Liverpool, Ohio" printed near the base. $150.00–200.00.
Wetzel Collection.

Meredith's Diamond Club Pure Rye, 8¼"h, quart, with "1880" printed at base. $150.00–200.00.
Wetzel Collection.

Mike & Jim's Private Stock 1881 Pure Rye Whiskey, 8¼" h, quart. $200.00–250.00.
Wetzel Collection.

Old Maryland, quart size,
labeling printed in brown.
$200.00–250.00.
Wetzel Collection.

Old Maryland 1881 Pure Rye Whiskey,
G. Riesmeyer St. Louis, Mo. Distilling Co.,
printed in lavender, 8" h, quart.
$200.00–250.00.
Wetzel Collection.

Pennsylvania Club Pure
Rye Whiskey, 8¼" h,
quart, labeling printed in
red. $250.00–300.00.
Wetzel Collection.

Pennsylvania Club quart size with
labeling printed in green.
$250.00–300.00.
Wetzel Collection.

Spring Lake Hand Made Sour Mash Bourbon, 8¼" h, quart, pink lettering.
$200.00–250.00.
Wetzel Collection.

Spring Lake quart size with label printed in light blue.
$200.00–250.00.
Wetzel Collection.

Spring Lake quart size with green printed label; original cork.
$200.00–250.00.
Wetzel Collection.

Urban Club Sour Mash Bourbon, A. Urban & Son, Quincy, ILL., 8¼" h, quart; original cork with ring handle.
$225.00–275.00.
Wetzel Collection.

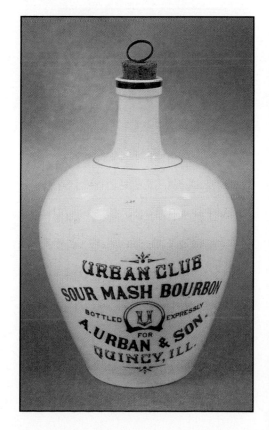

113

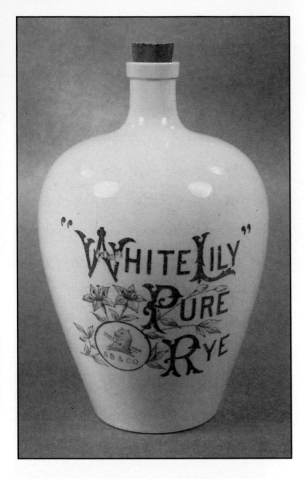

White Lily Pure Rye with "S. B. & Co. Trademark" (Steinhardt Bros.), 8¼" h, quart. $225.00–275.00.
Wetzel Collection.

White Lily Pure Rye, 8¼" h, quart; label printed in a reddish-brown. $225.00–275.00.
Estell Collection.

Gift Jug, 5¼" h, "Holiday Greetings," printed in green. $275.00–325.00.
Estell Collection.

Watch Fobs in the shape of whiskey jugs made as advertising souvenirs for Meredith Whiskey, 1¼" h, unmarked. $350.00–450.00 each.
Wetzel Collection.

Whiskey Jug, quart size; transfer portrait decoration of bust of woman in a filmy gown with flowers in her hair; the jug has a silver applied finish on body surrounding portrait. $400.00–500.00.
Daily Collection.

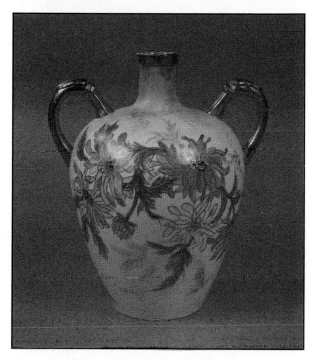

Whiskey Jug, quart size, two handles; hand-painted yellow and lavender-pink flowers outlined in gold; gold sponged work around neck, gold trim. $350.00–450.00.
Estell Collection.

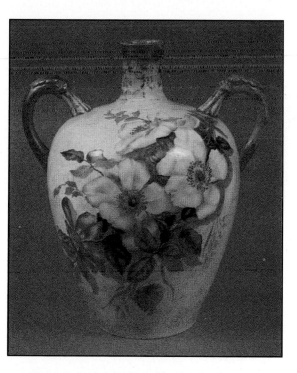

Whiskey Jug, two handles, quart size; hand-painted red and blue flowers with green leaves; gold outlining of shapes and gold enamel work on center of flowers; light pink finish on body, gold trim. $350.00–450.00.
Wetzel Collection.

Whiskey Jug, double handle, quart size; hand-painted white dogwood with one red blossom, green leaves, gold trim, signed "M.K.N. 1892," non-factory decoration; $300.00–400.00.
Wetzel Collection.

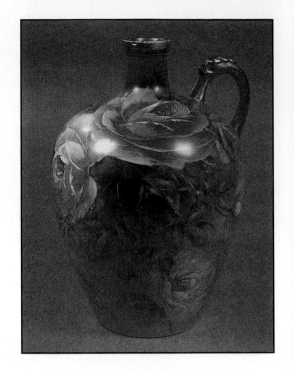

Whiskey Jug, quart size; hand-painted
corn decoration finished with a
lustrous high glaze; a dried corn
cob serves as the stopper.
$400.00–500.00.
Wetzel Collection.

Whiskey Jug, quart size; large
hand-painted roses, gold trim.
$350.00–450.00.
Wetzel Collection.

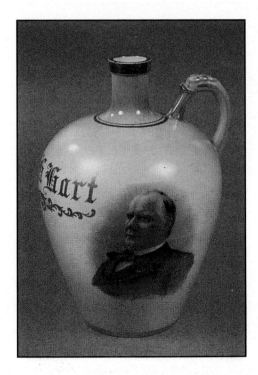

Whiskey Jug, quart size; hand-painted pink and yellow flowers; a black finish overlaid with gold designs
on neck, handle, and base of body; signed "J.E.B.
2/92," non-factory decoration.
$350.00–450.00.
Estell Collection.

Whiskey Jug, quart size; transfer portrait of William
McKinley with "Will H. Hart" (owner of jug) printed
in gold on the body; pink finish, gold trim.
$500.00–600.00.
Wetzel Collection.

Whiskey Jug, quart size; hand-painted large pink flowers with small lavender-blue flowers, gold trim, matte finish. $350.00–450.00.
Wetzel Collection.

Whiskey Jug, quart size; hand-painted yellow daisies on blue background. $300.00–$400.00.
Wetzel Collection.

Whiskey Jug, quart size; large yellow hand-painted floral decor with green leaves; neck and handle painted gold; signed "B.D.R. 91 Xmas," non-factory decoration. $300.00–400.00.
Wetzel Collection.

Whiskey Jug, quart size; large golden-yellow flowers and buds with slender green leaves, gold trim; signed "Brown," non-factory decoration. $300.00–400.00.
Wetzel Collection.

Whiskey Jug, quart size; hand-painted lavender floral decoration, gold trim.
$300.00–400.00.

Whiskey Jug, quart size; hand-painted red flowers with shapes outlined in gold; black finish on neck; matte body finish. The lettering of "Spring Lake Distilling" is visible under the hand-painted floral decoration, non-factory decoration.
$250.00–300.00.
Riggs Collection.

Whiskey Jug, quart size; hand-painted pink flowers and green leaves with gold sponged work on body, matte body finish. This decoration is very similar to that shown on the first hand-painted, two-handled jug.
$350.00–450.00.
Wetzel Collection.

Whiskey Jug, quart size; large hand–painted green leaves with small pink buds, non-factory decoration.
$300.00–350.00.
Estell Collection.

Whiskey Jug, quart size; small hand-painted pink flowers with white enameled centers on white background decorate top third of jug with a blue finish on the lower two-thirds of body; gold enameled scroll work divides the two sections. $300.00–400.00.
Wetzel Collection.

Whiskey Jug, quart size; hand-painted lavender flowers; neck and handle painted gold. $300.00–400.00.
Wetzel Collection.

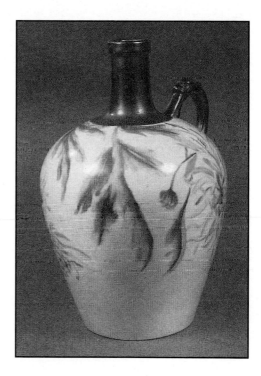

Whiskey Jug, quart size; hand-painted lavender and yellow flowers form a border around top portion of jug's body; green leaves on a gray background painted on the neck and top of jug, non-factory decoration. $300.00–350.00.
Wetzel Collection.

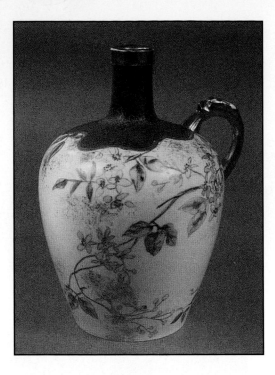

Whiskey Jug, quart size; small hand-painted pink flowers with green leaves on body; the neck has a dark green finish overlaid with gold designs, non-factory decoration. $300.00–350.00.
Wetzel Collection.

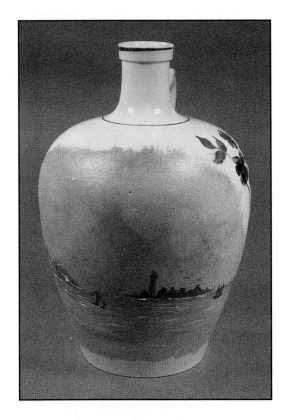

Whiskey Jug, quart size, hand-painted ocean scene on one side of jug with hand-painted flowers on the reverse, non-factory decoration. $325.00–375.00.
Wetzel Collection.

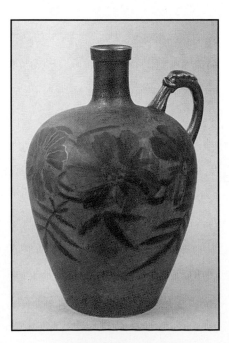

Whiskey Jug, quart size, blue monochrome hand-painted flowers and background with gold outlining of shapes and gold sponged work on neck; matte finish, non-factory decoration. $250.00–300.00.
Estell Collection.

II.
K. T. & K. CALIFORNIA

Marks

Decorative and Novelty China

Marks

1. K. T. & K. Calif. Hand MadE mark, incised, circa 1937–1948. (Note that the "M" in Hand MadE" is upside down; the "n" in "Hand" is also sometimes found in this manner; and the "E" in "MadE" is always in upper case form. This style of writing was used by Eileen Taylor, and thus marks with the upside down "M" and the upper case "E" at the end, indicate that Eileen marked the piece of pottery.)

2. K. T. &. K. Handmade, California, incised script mark, circa 1937–1948. This mark is in Pearl Taylor's handwriting.

3. KTK S—V CHINA, incised printed mark, circa 1937–1948.

4. K.T. & K. incised printed letters with "Burbank" incised in script form, circa 1937–1948.

The following photographs are marked with one of the marks on page 122 or a variation of one of those marks. Mark photographs by Chris Crain.

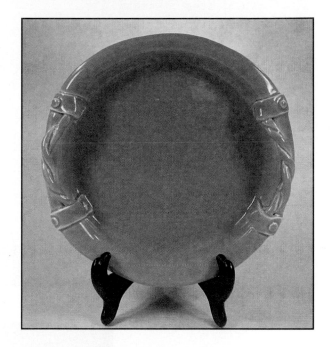

Bowl with an irregularly scalloped border and leaf shaped design on exterior, turquoise finish. This piece was made by Pearl Taylor, wife of Homer J. Taylor. The mark on this bowl is shown in the third photo of the California marks on page 122.
$40.00–50.00.
Crain Collection.

Bowl, 9" d, turquoise finish; rolled rim with applied rope design for handles.
$70.00–80.00.
Wetzel Collection.

Vase, turquoise finish; scalloped neck with front half rolled down; applied flower and stem with a large incised leaf on front.
$45.00–55.00.
Crain Collection.

Pair of Vases, 4¾" h x 3" w, with matching Bowl, 4" h x 6" d; light blue glaze sprayed with a dusty rose color; applied floral shapes and incised leaves.
Bowl, $80.00–100.00.
Vases, pair, $120.00–140.00.
Wetzel Collection.

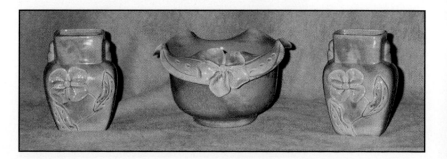

Leaf Dish, 6" d; light blue glaze sprayed with a raspberry-colored finish; this piece is initialed "H" for Homer J. Taylor.
$30.00–40.00.
Crain Collection.

Divided Dish with applied flowers and stems forming center handle; decorated with the same blue and raspberry colors as in preceding picture. The following three pieces also have this same finish.
$55.00–65.00.
Crain Collection.

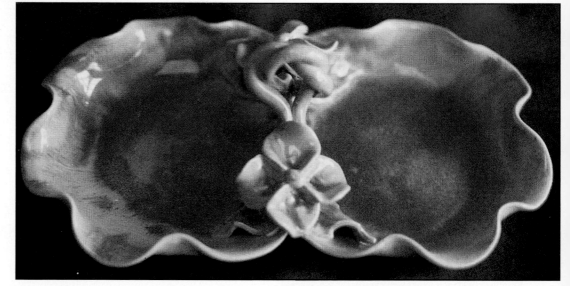

Candle Holder; scalloped body in bowl form with holder placed in center.
$25.00–30.00.
Crain Collection.

Basket with applied twisted rope handle and bow.
$35.00–45.00.
Crain Collection.

Pitcher, 6¼" h; curved sectional body design with
twisted rope style handle; signed "Eileen 1/21/43."
$50.00–60.00.
Crain Collection.

Vase, 4½" h; fancy bow applied to front of neck;
"S" initial incised with mark.
$55.00–65.00.
Wetzel Collection.

Handled Basket, 7½" 1 x 5½" h; the raspberry color is
more visible on this and the following four examples.
$35.00–45.00.
Wetzel Collection.

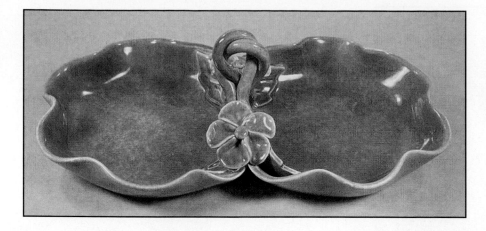

Divided Dish, 10¾" 1 x 5" h.
$55.00–65.00.
Wetzel Collection.

Creamer, 2½" h, and Open Sugar Bowl, 2½" h,
with the same applied floral shape as on
other pieces, serving as handles.
$50.00–60.00 pair.
Wetzel Collection.

Vase, 6" h, ovoid body with round neck; intialed "H" for Homer Taylor.
$40.00–50.00.
Wetzel Collection.

Vase, 5¼" h x 5¼" w, square shape in a late Art Deco style.
$45.00–55.00.
Wetzel Collection.

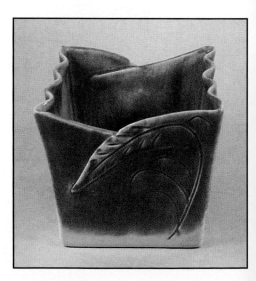

Creamer, 2½" h and Open Sugar Bowl, 2½" h;
yellow monochrome finish.
$50.00–60.00, pair.
Wetzel Collection.

Creamer, 2½" h, and Open Sugar Bowl, 1¾" h;
peach monochrome finish; twisted rope
handles and dimple marks on body.
$60.00–70.00, pair.
Wetzel Collection.

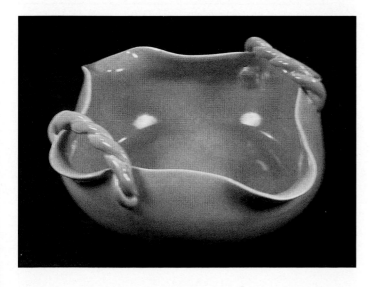

Bowl, 3¼" h x 8½" w; peach monochrome finish; twisted
rope handles on top of bowl on each side.
$80.00–90.00.
Wetzel Collection.

Flower Floater or Bowl with applied bow on rim, 13" 1 x 7" w; dark blue glaze with hints of black which keeps the overall look quite dark, but is not a true solid color. This finish was apparently quite popular for many examples are found with this decoration. Some examples are shown in the following 15 photographs.
$55.00–65.00.
Wetzel Collection.

Flower Floater, 13" 1 x 8" w; this example has two applied bows; pair of Candle Holders, 3" h, with applied bow on front.
Flower Floater, $65.00–75.00.
Candle Holders, pair, $40.00–50.00.
Wetzel Collection.

Bowl, 9" d; deeply scalloped border with applied calla lilies on one side.
$40.00–50.00.
Wetzel Collection.

Watering Can, 3" h, designed to hold cigarettes;
and Wheelbarrow, 3" h, designed to hold matches.
$30.00–40.00 each.
Wetzel Collection.

Boot, 6¼" h; the initial "H" (for Homer J. Taylor)
is incised with the mark.
$50.00–60.00.
Wetzel Collection.

Vase, 6¼" h; abstract overlapping line design
on body; "S S" Intials incised with mark.
$35.00–45.00.
Wetzel Collection.

Pear, 6" 1 with hollowed interior and opening below
applied leaf handle; "S" initial incised with mark.
$40.00–50.00.
Wetzel Collection.

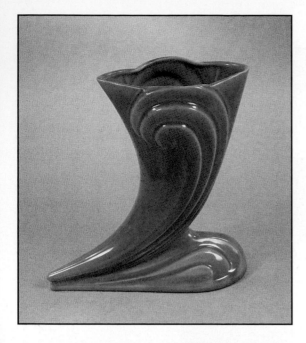

Vase, 5½" h; applied pear and
leaves decorate front.
$50.00–60.00.
Crain Collection.

Cornacopia Vase, 7½" h; stylized abstract
design on body and base.
This example has California Mark 3 plus
"California" as part of the mark.
$80.00–90.00.
Wetzel Collection.

Pitcher, 4" h; three sections form a rounded body and flared
neck with twisted rope style handle; artist signed "B" for
Bonnie Taylor Wollard, another daughter of Homer J. Taylor.
$45.00–55.00.
Crain Collection.

Vase, 4" h; fancy bow design applied to front of vase;
artist signed "D" for Dubby Davidson, Eileen Taylor's
second husband, a son-in-law of Homer J. Taylor.
$45.00–55.00.
Crain Collection.

Dutch Shoe, 4" l x 2½" w.
$40.00–50.00.
Crain Collection.

Wall Pocket, 9" w, made in the form of a hat
and pierced on the back for hanging.
$35.00–45.00.
Crain Collection.

Basket, 8" l x 6½" w, rope handle.
$30.00–40.00.
Crain Collection.

Two Sugar Bowls with slightly different body
shapes and a variation in the number of petals
on the flowers decorating the pieces.
$50.00–60.00, pair.
Crain Collection.

Flower Floater, 10½" d; deeply fluted pie crust style border; this piece has Califronia Mark 4 with –"Burbank" incised as part of the mark. This is the only known example with this particular mark.
$45.00–55.00.
Crain Collection.

Flower Holder, 4" h x 7½" w; a diamond shaped body with elaborate floral designs; pedestal base. This example has California Mark 3.
$80.00–100.00.
Crain Collection.

Rooster, 6" h, with hollow interior; these also were made in blue and yellow-green.
$65.00–75.00.
Crain Collection.

Pair of Candle Holders, 3" h; the basic color is chartreuse with a brown color sprayed over it to produce a mottled appearance. The following four photographs show a similar decoration.
$80.00–100.00, pair.
Wetzel Collection.

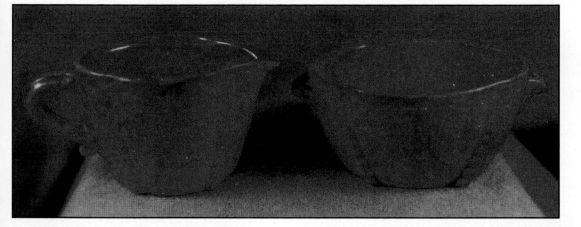

Creamer, 2½" h and Open
Sugar Bowl, 2" h; marked
"KT&K Cabaña Calif."
45.00-55.00, pair.
Crain Collection.

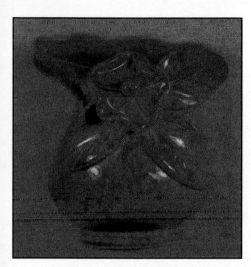

Vase, 4" h; applied flower
and leaves on front.
$55.00–65.00.
Crain Collection.

Wall Pockets in the shape of women's faces
with a fancy headdress, 7¾" 1.
$125.00–150.00, pair.
Wetzel Collection.

Sugar Bowl, 2" h x 3½" w
and handled Basket,
7" 1 x 5" w.
Sugar Bowl, $25.00–30.00.
Basket, $40.00–50.00.
Crain Collection.

Bowl, 6" 1 x 5½" w; decorated with a pale red glaze highlighted with blue; applied bow and ribbon. $40.00–50.00.
Crain Collection.

Bowl, 7" d; 3" h; two sides are deeply cut and outer border is rolled to form handles. $35.00–45.00.
Crain Collection.

Vase, 5½" h x 5½" w, square shape; lightly incised abstract leaf design. This particular style of vase is attributed exclusively to Eileen Taylor. $40.00–50.00.
Crain Collection.

Bowl, 5" h x 6" w x 6" l, a diamond shape with deeply scalloped border and applied bow and ribbon handle. $50.00–60.00.
Crain Collection.

Dutch Shoe, 7½" l x 3½" h; incised initial "C" with mark. $40.00–50.00.
Crain Collection.

Wall Pocket with matte blue monochrome glaze; applied flowers, stems, and leaves form a simple body design. $45.00–55.00.
Crain Collection.

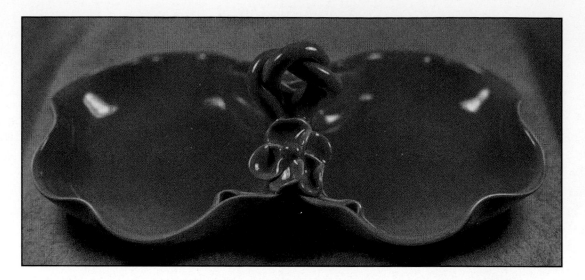

Divided Dish with applied flowers and twisted vine shaped center handle.
This decorative glaze has a light green base sprayed with a light brown color to produce
a "sea foam" effect. This piece and the following seven photographs are in this color.
$45.00–55.00.
Crain Collection.

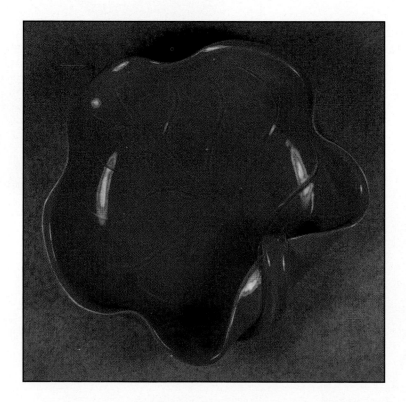

Leaf Dish, 6" w; artist signed "L" which may indicate
Lee Brooks, an employee.
$30.00–40.00.
Crain Collection.

Shallow Dish, 8" w x1¾" d; applied bow.
$35.00–45.00.
Crain Collection.

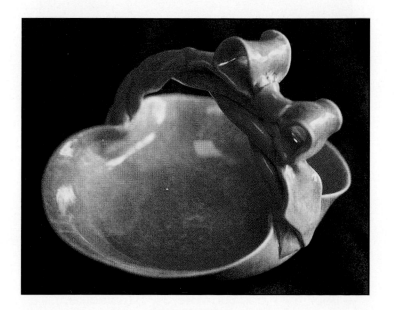

Basket with bow and rope handle.
$35.00–45.00.
Crain Collection.

Duck Planter, 4½" h and Vase, 5" h with flower and leaf handles.
Duck, $50.00–60.00.
Vase, $45.00–55.00.
Crain Collection.

Boot, 6¼" h and Bud Vase, 3¾" h (unmarked).
Boot, $50.00–60.00.
Vase, $15.00–20.00.
Crain Collection.

Vase, 4½" h; applied flower and leaves decorate front of vase; artist initialed "S."
$45.00–55.00.
Wetzel Collection.

Flower Floater or Bowl, 12½" l x 4½" h; artist initialed "C."
$40.00–50.00.
Wetzel Collection.

Bowl, 6" d x 1½" d; pear and leaves decor; artist initial "M" on base.
$40.00–50.00.
Crain Collection.

Centerpiece Vase with three flower holders on pedestal base, 5¼" h x 10¼" w at top; all white, marked "KT&K cabaña Calif." $50.00–60.00.
Crain Collection.

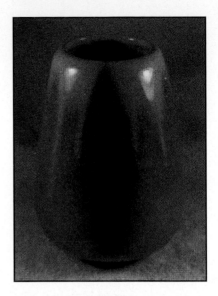

Vase, 4¼" h, several shades of green in an abstract pattern decorate body; no applied work. $40.00–50.00.
Crain Collection.

Duck Planter with applied bonnet; initialed "E" for Eileen Taylor who painted the piece. $50.00–60.00.
Crain Collection.

Small boy figure with barrel attached to back; this, like the preceding duck, could have been used for flowers or ivy or just as small "catch alls." $35.00–45.00.
Crain Collection.

Lamb figure with applied bow around neck.
$30.00–40.00.
Crain Collection.

Vase, 10½" h, bird with tree branches formed in
relief on body; light raspberry glaze overall;
incised mark of "KTK" over "California."
This piece may possibly be attributed to the
Harold Homer Knowles Pottery which
operated in Santa Clara, California, in 1923.
$125.00–150.00.
Wetzel Collection.

Train and car; the car holds ceramic coasters;
intialed "E" for Eileen Taylor who painted the set.
$100.00–125.00 set.
Crain Collection.

APPENDICES

K. T. & K. Original Molds

View of K. T. & K. Plant

Catalog Page for K. T. & K. Belleek Porcelain

Catalog Pages for K. T. & K. Lotus Ware China

Catalog Pages for K. T. & K. Hotel China

Advertisement for K. T. & K. Hotel China

K. T. & K. Brochure for "Little Gem Dinner Set"

Isaac W. Knowles Family Tree

Photographs of Col. John N. Taylor and Bellvina Taylor

Photograph of Bellvina Knowles Taylor

Views of John N. and Bellvina Taylor's Home

Letter to John N. Taylor from William McKinley, Jr.

Letter to Belle Taylor from Lou McKinley

Book Inscription to Homer Taylor from William McKinley, Jr.

Letter of Introduction for Homer J. Taylor from William McKinley, Jr.

Photographs of Homer J. Taylor

"KATEKAY" WADS

Letterhead for Knowles, Taylor & Knowles

Photographs of Eileen Taylor

APPENDIX 1

K. T. & K. Original Molds

A selection of KT&K molds and models made during the 1880–1890 era are shown
in the following photographs. Some examples of china made from the molds are also included.
All pieces are from the Wetzel Collection.

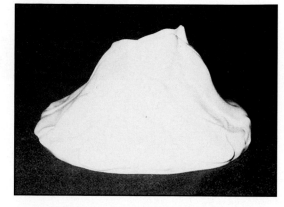

b. Example made from the model.

a. Model for base of Lily Vase which was made in
both a Belleek and a Lotus Ware body.

d. Example of small part of Lily Vase.

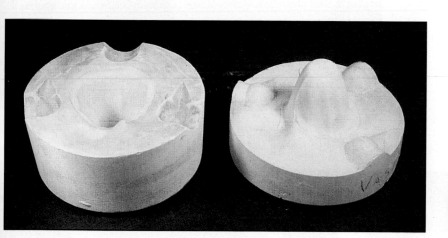

c. Model and Mold for small part of Lily Vase.

f. Example of Cup.

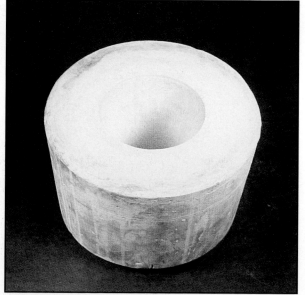

e. Cup Mold with straight sides and ribbed
design.

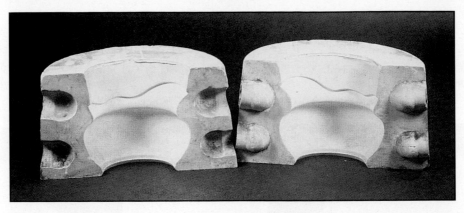

g. Mold for a Creamer.

h. Example of Creamer.

i. Bell Mold with an example, 5" h.

j. Mold for Shell Dish.

k. Example of Shell Dish, 16" x 15"

l. A Shell Mold with an example.

m. Mold for Cabbage Leaf Oval Bowl, large size.

n. Mold for a smaller size of the Cabbage Leaf Oval Bowl.

o. Examples of the Cabbage Leaf Oval Bowl in large and small sizes.

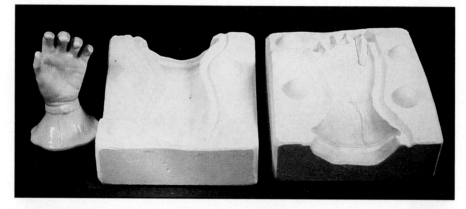

p. Mold and example for Small Hand, 5¾" h; note that the thumb piece was a separate mold (not shown).

q. Mold and example for Large Hand, 7½" h.

r. Decorative Plaque Mold, 14" 1 x 11¼" w; woman and cherub design.

s. Back of preceding Mold with the artist's signature and date.

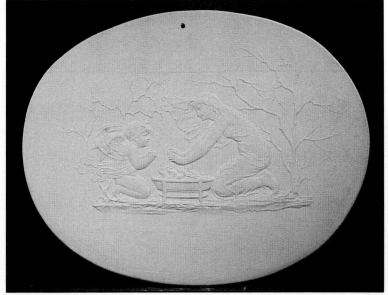

t. Example of the finished plaque made from the above mold.

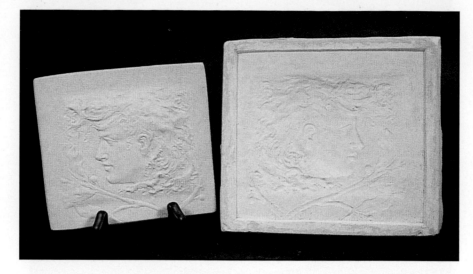

u. Plaque Mold, 6" sq. with face of a small boy; the smaller size shows the finished piece.

v. Plaque Mold for William McKinley,
14" 1 x 11" w.

w. Example of finished McKinley Plaque.

APPENDIX 2

View of K. T. & K. Plant

View of the Knowles, Taylor & Knowles plant as shown on their *Souvenir* brochure.
This brochure is not dated but is after 1893; an original brochure from the Wetzel Collection.

APPENDIX 3

Catalog page for K. T. & K. Belleek Porcelain

A page from a Knowles, Taylor & Knowles catalog illustrating examples of their Belleek production.
The original page from this catalog is at the East Liverpool, Ohio, Ceramic Museum.
The page is circa 1889; copy from the Wetzel Collection.

79. Shell Tray, No. 3.	89. Melon Tea Pot.	99. Roman Jug, 12s.
80. Cactus Tea Pot.	90. Globe Jugs, 30s and 24s.	100. Vase Roman.
81. Cactus Sugar.	91. Venice Cream.	101. Shell Trays, No. 1 and 2.
82. Cactus Cream.	92. Venice Sugar.	102. Rose Jar, handled, No. 1.
83. Cactus Tea and Saucer.	93. Globe After Dinner Coffee and Saucer.	103. Shell, shell foot.
84. Cactus After Dinner Coffee and Saucer.	94. Globe Tea and Saucer.	104. Gipsy Kettle.
85. Melon After Dinner Coffee and Saucer.	95. Globe Cream, 36s.	105. Grecian Ewer, No. 1.
86. Melon Tea and Saucer.	96. Globe Sugar.	106. Tusk Jugs, 36s, 30s, 24s and 12s.
87. Melon Cream.	97. Globe Tea Pot.	107. Rose Jar, No 2.
88. Melon Sugar.	98. Vase Lily.	108. Washington Jugs, 36s, 30s, 12s, 6s and 4s.

APPENDIX 4

Catalog pages for Lotus Ware China

Four pages from the Knowles, Taylor & Knowles Company catalog illustrating their Lotus Ware production. The pages are not dated, but they would have been published during the early 1890s. The pages shown here are copies made from one of the original KT&K salesman's catalogs. The catalog contained thirteen pages. This catalog portrays examples for Hotel China also which are shown in another appendix. The catalog is from the Wetzel Collection.

201. Shell Trays, 1s, 2s, 3s, 4s.
203. Lotus Tea.
204. Cosmo Tea.
206. Venis Teapot, Sugar and Cream.
207. Davenport Teapot, Sugar and Cream.
208. Quincy Chocolate Jug.
209. Etruscan Vase.

210. Roman Vase.
211. Lily Vase.
212. Venetian Vase.
213. Grecian Vase.
214. Flower Bowl.
228. Mecca A.D. Coffee Cup and Saucer.
229. Hindoo Tea (small) Cup and Saucer.

230. Etruscan Ewer.
231. Winona Chocolate Jug.
232. Egyptian Vase.
233. Ionian Vase.
234. Savonian Vase.
235. Fan Pin Tray.

Appendix 4 — Catalog pages for Lotus Ware China

215. Tuscan Vase.
216. Tuscan Vase.
217. Tuscan Vase.
218. Tuscan Vase.
242. Tuscan Vase.
219. Columbia Bowl.
220. Columbia Bowl.

221. Columbia Bowl.
222. Columbia Bowl.
223. Columbia Bowl.
224. Columbia Bowl.
236. Columbia Bowl.
237. Columbia Bowl.
238. Columbia Bowl.

225. Cracker Jar.
226. Cracker Jar.
227. Cracker Jar.
239. Orleans Rose Jar.
240. Avignon Rose Jar.
241. Persian Rose Jar.
243. Leaf Bon-bon.

244. Globe Teapot, Sugar and Cream.
245. Globe Jugs, 24s, 30s, 36s, 42s.
246. Valenciennes Teapot, Sugar and Cream.
247. Valenciennes Jugs, 24s, 30s, 36s, 42s.
248. Etruscan Ewer.
249. Chestnut Sugar and Cream.
252. Perfume Ewer.

250. Rustic Jardiniere, 10".
251. Rustic Jardiniere, 8".
253. Individual Salts.
254. Coral Photo Holder.
255. Sonoma Tea.
256. Oriental A.D. Coffee.

Appendix 4 — Catalog pages for Lotus Ware China

264. Laconian Vase.
257. Laconian Vase, filigreed.
279. Arcanian Vase.
270. Etruscan Vase, filigreed.
272. Etruscan Vase, filigreed.
275. Egyptian Vase, filigreed.
281. Ionian Vase, filigreed.

276. Tuscan Vase.
277. Tuscan Vase.
280. Tuscan Vase.
268. Etruscan Ewer, filigreed.
274. Etruscan Ewer, filigreed.
258. Finger Bowl.

263. Oatmeal Nappie.
260. Bon Nappies, 5½", 6½", 8".
262. Jewel Box, filigree cover.
259. Autun Jar, filigree handles.
261. Ivica Jar, filigree cover.
269. Deccan Jar, filigreed.

273. Luxor Jar, triangular filigree.
265. Shell Salad.
266. Orange Dish.
267. Shell Salad, coral foot.
271. Fern Jardineire, 8".
278. Fern Jardineire, 10".

Appendix 4 — Catalogs page for Lotus Ware China

279. Arcanian Vase, white.
283. Syrian Vase, white.
284. Leaf Jug, white.
285. Cremonian Vase, white.
286. Parmian Vase, white.
287. Thebian Vase, white.
288. Umbrian Vase, white.
289. Syrian Vase, white.

500. Parmian Vase, white flowers on celadon body.
500. Parmian Vase, white flowers on olive body.
501. Thebian Vase, white flowers on celadon body.
501. Thebian Vase, white flowers on olive body.
502. Umbrian Vase, white flowers on celadon body.
502. Umbrian Vase, white flowers on olive body.
503. Etruscan Ewer, white flowers on celadon body.
503. Etruscan Ewer, white flowers on olive body.

504. Arcanian Vase, white flowers on celadon body.
504. Arcanian Vase, white flowers on olive body.
505. Syrian Vase, white flowers on celadon body
505. Syrian Vase, white flowers on olive body.
506. Tiberian Ewer, white flowers on celadon body.
506. Tiberian Ewer, white flowers on olive body.
507. Cremonian Vase, white flowers on celadon body.
507. Cremonian Vase, white flowers on olive body.

508. Grecian Vase, white flowers on celadon body.
508. Grecian Vase, white flowers on olive body.
509. Columbia Bowl, white flowers on celadon body.
509. Columbia Bowl, white flowers on olive body.
510. Roman Vase, white flowers on celadon body.
510. Roman Vase, white flowers on olive body.
511. Venetian Vase, white flowers on celadon body.
511. Venetian Vase, white flowers on olive body.

APPENDIX 5

Catalog pages for K. T. & K. Hotel China

ILLUSTRATIONS
—OF—

HOTEL CHINA.

Preserve this and Insert Additional Illustrations Sent Hereafter.

SIMMS NEW PROCESS COLOR PRINT,

Cover and remaining nine pages of
the Knowles, Taylor & Knowles
catalog, circa early 1890s.
Wetzel Collection.

1. Small Sauce Boat.	7. Rocaille, Jugs 42s to 4s.	12½. Individual Cream, Vienna, I.
2. Hotel Butter, loose drainer.	8. Spice Stand, four compartments.	13. Individual Cream, Rocaille, 2.
3. Hotel Butter, fast drainer.	9. Individual B. & T. Cream, I.	14. Bell Boy Jugs, 24s and 12s.
4. Ice Tub.	10. Individual Cream, double spout, I.	15. Bell Boy Jugs, 24s and 12s.
5. Cracker Jar.	11. Individual Cream, solid handle, I.	16. Rocaille Ice Jugs, 6s and 4s.
6. Cake Cover, pierced.	12. Individual Cream, plain, oval, I.	

Items 1 through 16.

17. Fruit Saucers, 4 and 5 inch.
19. Plates, ½ thick, 5 to 8 inch.
20. Individual Butter, 2½ inch.
21. Plates, deep, thick, 6, 7 and 8 inch.
22. Plates, thick 5, 6, 7 and 8 inch.
23. Shell Ice Cream.
24. Ice Creams, 3½, 4 and 5 inch.
25. Ice Creams, ½ thick, 3½, 4 and 5 inch.
28. Bowl Coffee, handled and unhandled.
30. Plain Mugs, 42s and 24s.

32. Double Egg Cup.
33. Single Egg Cup, footed.
34. Saxon, after dinner, handled Coffee.
35. Conic handled Coffee.
36. Saxon handled Coffee, ½ thick.
37. Tulip Coffees handled and unhandled.
38. Extra Coffees, handled and unhandled.
39. Saxon Coffees, handled and unhandled.
40. Saxon Tea, handled.

41. Custard, footed, unhandled.
42. Hotel Covered Mustard.
43. Handled and Covered Mustard.
44. Oyster Bowls, low foot, 30s and 24s.
45. Oyster Bowls, 36s, 30s and 24s.
46. Bowl, Individual Sugar.
47. Bowl, Individual Sugar, covered.
48. Vienna Sugars, 42s, 36s, 30s and 24s.
49. Box Sugars, 42s, 36s, 30s and 24s.

Items 17 through 49.

52. Oyster Nappies, 42s, 36s, 30s, 24s.
53. Nappies, 3 inch to 9 inch.
54. Bakers, 2½ inch to 8 inch.
55. Bakers, wide, 3 and 4 inch.

56. Salads, 6, 7, 8 and 9 inch.
57. Shell Pickle.
58. Vierzon Comport, 8 inch.
59. Home Covered Butter.

60. Plain Comports, 6, 7, 8 and 9 inch.
61. Dishes, thick, 2½ to 12 inch
    13 to 16 inch, ½ thick.

Items 52 through 61.

156

62. Hotel Cuspidor, handled and covered 2s.
63. Hotel Parlor Spittoon.
64. Large Fancy Spittoon.
65. Cable Cuspidor, open and unhandled, 2s.
66. Door Knob.

67. Oval Soap Slab.
68. Boston Soap.
69. Hanging Soap.
70. Match Safes, 1s, 2s, 3s.
72. Insulators, cleat, small.

73. Hotel Cuspidor, open and unhandled, 2s.
74. Square Soap.
75. Square Soap Slab.
76. Hotel Covered Chamber.
77. Hotel Ewer and Basin.

Items 62 through 77.

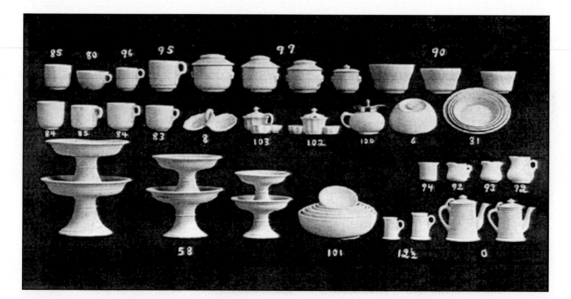

85. J. D. & S. unhandled Teas, ½ thick.
85. J. D. & S. handled Teas, thick.
80. New York K. & T. handled Coffee, ½ thick.
96. A. D. Culot handled Coffee, thick.
95. Culot handled Coffee, thick.
84. Philadelphia handled Tea, extra ½ thick.
84. Philadelphia handled Tea, ½ thick.
83. Philadelphia handled Tea, ½ thick.
99. Round Sugars, thick, 36s, 30s and 24s.

99. Round Sugars, Restaurant, thick.
90. Tulip Bowls, thick 36s, 30s and 24s.
8. Spice Stand, toe compartments.
103. Salt, Pepper and Mustard, handled.
102. Salt, Pepper and Mustard.
100. Globe Molasses Can.
6. Buckwheat Cake Cover with Knob and Pierced.
81. Oyster Plates, ½ thick, 5, 5¾, 6½, 7¼ in.

58. Vierzon Comports, thick, 5, 6, 7, 8, 8½ and 9 inch.
101. Globe Nappies, 3, 4, 5, 6, 7, 8 and 9 inch 12½ inch Vienna Ind. Creams, 1s and 2s.
94. G. H. M. Double-Lipped Cream, 1s.
92. Saxon Creams, 1s and 2s.
93. Saxon Double-Spout Cream, 1s.
0. Vienna Coffee and Teapot, Ind., 1s and 2s.

Items 85 through 100.
(Notice some missing numbers from other pages are listed here,
and the numbers are not in numerical order.)

157

104. Harvard Spittoon.
105. Princeton Spittoon.
106. Half Thick Dishes, Limoges.
107. Half Thick Dishes, Pompadour.
108. H. & B. Bowl.
109. Chicago Oyster Nappie, 5 and 6 inch.
110. Open Round Sugar, thick.
111. Shirred Egg Dish.
112. 4 inch Pompadour Fruit.

113. Ind. Soup Tureen.
114. 30s, Rocaille Sugar.
115. Bakers, half thick, 2½ to 10 inchs.
116. Handled Broth Bowl and Stand.
117. Footed Match Stand.
118. Handled and Covered Mustard, N. Y.
119. Handled Custard
120. A. D. Coffee, Conic.
121. A. D. Coffee, Egg.

122. A. D. Coffee, Buffalo.
123. A. D. Coffee, Saxon, small.
124. Handled Baltimore Tea.
125. Unhandled Baltimore Tea.
126. 2s, Sauce Boat.
  1. 1s, Sauce Boat.
127. Columbus Covered Jug and Stand.
128. Pompadour Ind. Butter.
129. Ramican.

Items 104 through 129.

64. Fluted Spittoon.
64. Montana Spittoon.
16. Rocaille Ice Jug, 12s.

14. Bell Boy Jug, 30s.
98. Salads, low foot, plain, 5, 6, 7, 8 and 9 inch.

91. Punch Bowls, 9, 10, 11, 12½, 13½ and
   15 inch.
97. Ice Tubs with Hoops, 8 and 9 inch.

Other numbers not in numerical order.

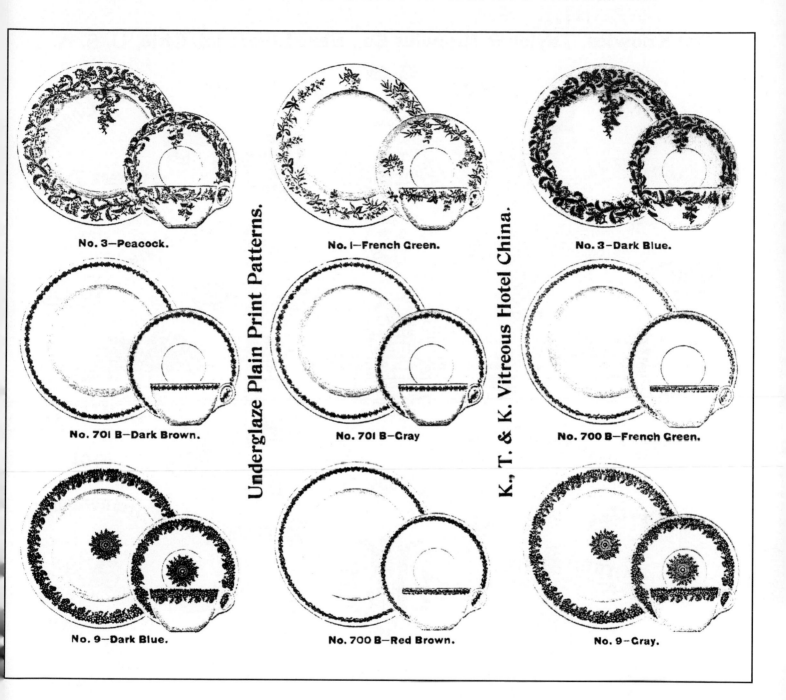

No. 3–Peacock.

No. 1–French Green.

No. 3–Dark Blue.

No. 701 B–Dark Brown.

No. 701 B–Gray

No. 700 B–French Green.

No. 9–Dark Blue.

No. 700 B–Red Brown.

No. 9–Gray.

Underglaze Plain Print Patterns.

K., T. & K. Vitreous Hotel China.

Underglaze printed patterns and available colors.

Assortment of logos, monograms, emblems, and names illustrating the
various ways commercial orders could be customized.

APPENDIX 6

Advertisement for K. T. & K. Hotel China

An early advertisement for Knowles, Taylor & Knowles hotel china; Collection of the East Liverpool, Ohio, Ceramic Museum.

APPENDIX 7

K. T. & K. Brochure for "Little Gem dinner Set."

Pages from a Knowles, Taylor & Knowles brochure for their children's china:
The Little Gem Dinner Set.
This brochure was found in Eileen Taylor's baby book. It was in a section labeled
"Spring 1911." Eileen was born on December 23, 1901.
The original pages are owned by Chris Crain. The copies are from the Wetzel Collection.

If you have a good stock of these "Little Gems" it will be very valuable to you

THE LITTLE GEM DINNER SET

THE KNOWLES, TAYLOR & KNOWLES COMPANY
THE LARGEST AND MOST RELIABLE POTTERS ANYWHERE
EAST LIVERPOOL, OHIO, U. S. A.

Title Page of Brochure.

THE LITTLE GEM DINNER SET
40 PIECES

¶ The Little Gem Dinner Set manufactured by us is made with the same workmanship and care that is used in producing our other high-class grades of goods. There are three decorations, Greenway Figures, Rose and Scroll and Pink Roses with Forget-me-nots.

¶ These Sets are designed for practical use for children, luncheons and sick trays. They are good anywhere and will sell the year round. They are packed each set separately in a corrugated paper carton at $2.70 net per set.

COMPOSITION				
6 Plates, 4 inch	6 Cups, A. D.	6 Ind. Butters	1 Baker, 3 inch	1 Sugar
6 Fruits, 3½ inch	6 Saucers	2 Dishes, 6 and 3 inch	1 Cream	2 Cov. Dishes

Picture and advertisement for the china.

APPENDIX 8

Issac W. Knowles Family Tree

The genealogy of Isaac W. Knowles by his first and second wives shows the relationships of the owners of the Knowles, Taylor & Knowles Company, compiled from historical information and family records from the Crain Collection. All birth and death dates were not available.

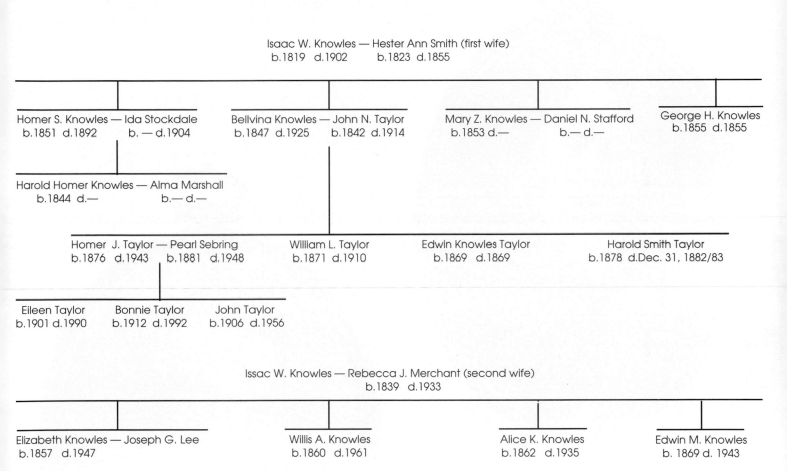

Isaac W. Knowles — Hester Ann Smith (first wife)
b.1819 d.1902   b.1823 d.1855

Homer S. Knowles — Ida Stockdale
b.1851 d.1892   b. — d.1904

Bellvina Knowles — John N. Taylor
b.1847 d.1925   b.1842 d.1914

Mary Z. Knowles — Daniel N. Stafford
b.1853 d.—   b.— d.—

George H. Knowles
b.1855 d.1855

Harold Homer Knowles — Alma Marshall
b.1844 d.—   b.— d.—

Homer J. Taylor — Pearl Sebring
b.1876 d.1943   b.1881 d.1948

William L. Taylor
b.1871 d.1910

Edwin Knowles Taylor
b.1869 d.1869

Harold Smith Taylor
b.1878 d.Dec. 31, 1882/83

Eileen Taylor
b.1901 d.1990

Bonnie Taylor
b.1912 d.1992

John Taylor
b.1906 d.1956

Isaac W. Knowles — Rebecca J. Merchant (second wife)
b.1839 d.1933

Elizabeth Knowles — Joseph G. Lee
b.1857 d.1947

Willis A. Knowles
b.1860 d.1961

Alice K. Knowles
b.1862 d.1935

Edwin M. Knowles
b. 1869 d. 1943

163

APPENDIX 9

Photographs of Col. John N. Taylor and Bellvina Taylor

Col. John N. Taylor, one of the original partners of the Knowles, Taylor & Knowles Company and his wife, daughter of Isaac W. Knowles, Bellvina "Belle" Knowles Taylor; Crain Collection.

APPENDIX 10

Photograph of Bellvina Knolwes Taylor

Bellvina "Belle" Catherine Knowles Taylor,
daughter of Knowles, Taylor & Knowles founder,
Isaac Knowles and wife of Col. John N. Taylor
partner of Isaac Knowles. Crain Collection.

APPENDIX 11

Views of John N. and Bellvina Taylor's home.

Col. John N. and Belle Taylor's home at 165 Sixth Street in East Liverpool, Ohio.
The Taylors purchased the house from Belle's brother, Homer H. Knowles
and his wife Clair when Knowles left East Liverpool to move to New York City.
The house was sold to the city after John N. Taylor died in 1914.
The city razed the building and built a City Hall on the location.

The first photograph was on a post card illustrating the Odd Fellow Temple in East Liverpool which was next to the Taylor home. The post card and the second photograph of the house were items from Eileen Taylor's baby albums. Photographs and information from the Crain Collection.

APPENDIX 12

Letter to John N. Taylor from William McKinley, Jr.

Letter from William McKinley to John N. Taylor, December 10, 1891,
asking Taylor to join the Governor's staff. John Taylor accepted the invitation and from then on,
he was addressed as "Colonel John N. Taylor." Crain Collection.

CANTON, OHIO

Dec 10. 1891

Col. John N. Taylor
East Liverpool, OH

My Dear Friend:

I beg to tender you a place on the Governor's Staff as Colonel and Aide de Camp I need not tell you that it will give me the greatest personal pleasure to have you take this place.

Sincerely Yours,

W M Kinley Jr

APPENDICES 13

Letter to Belle Taylor from Lou McKinley

Letter from Lou McKinley, William McKinley's wife, to Belle Taylor on November 30, 1892, extending sympathy to Mrs. Taylor on the death of her brother, Homer Knowles. Crain Collection.

STATE OF OHIO
EXECUTIVE CHAMBER
COLUMBUS

Dear Mrs Taylor:

Your note of 11th came and would have been answered earlier but for Father McKinley's illness and death, which you have noted.

I was so sorry to learn of your brother's death. Mr McKinley told me all about it upon his return from East Liverpool.

Your invitation to visit you, I appreciate, and whenever we can, I shall be glad to drop in and see you. Cato McWilliam's address is 3961 Lake Ave, Chicago. With kind regards to Mr Taylor, believe me

Yours sincerely

Lou S McKinley

30 Nov-92-

APPENDIX 14

Book Inscription to Homer Taylor from William McKinley, Jr.

Inscription and autograph of Mr. and Mrs. McKinley on December 25, 1894, on the title page of a book, *The Presidents of the United States, 1789–1894.* The book was inscribed "For Homer <u>Knowles</u> Taylor," although his name was Homer J. Taylor. Crain Collection.

THE PRESIDENTS
OF THE UNITED STATES

If you would understand history, study men
CHARLES KINGSLEY

APPENDIX 15

Letter of Introduction for Homer J. Taylor from William McKinley, Jr.

Letter of Introduction from President William McKinley on December 19, 1899,
for Homer Taylor to present on his trip around the world. Crain Collection.

EXECUTIVE MANSION,
WASHINGTON.

December 19, 1899.

TO WHOM IT MAY CONCERN:

I take great pleasure in bespeaking for Mr.
Homer Taylor, of East Liverpool, Ohio, who is making
a trip around the world, the usual courtesies of our
diplomatic and consular representatives and of others
whom he may meet upon his journey.

William McKinley

APPENDIX 16

Photographs of Homer J. Taylor

Homer J. Taylor, son of Col. John N. Taylor; Homer served as President of the Knowles, Taylor & Knowles Company from after the death of his father in 1914 until the company closed in 1929. Homer J. Taylor founded the Burbank, California, KT&K Pottery circa 1937. Crain Collection.

APPENDIX 17

"KATEKAY WADS"

Cover page of a "KATEKAY" WAD. These were small four page tracts designed to fit into a pottery worker's pay envelope. They served as a type of newsletter where the owner put forth his views and philosophies of the world and the times. "KATEKAY" was also the cable address code used by Western Union for the company. (See the letterhead in the following appendix.) The "KATEKAY" WADS are not dated. From the information concerning various world events which is discussed in them, however, it appears that they were written during Homer J. Taylor's tenure as president of the company. Crain Collection.

APPENDIX 18

Letterhead for Knowles, Taylor & Knowles

Letterhead when Homer J. Taylor was president of the
Knowles, Taylor & Knowles Company in East Liverpool, Ohio. Note cable address is
"KATEKAY."
A New York Office was located at 1107 Broadway. Crain Collection.

ESTABLISHED 1854

THE KNOWLES, TAYLOR AND KNOWLES COMPANY

Manufacturing Potters and Decorators

EAST LIVERPOOL OHIO

CABLE ADDRESS "KATEKAY"
WESTERN UNION CODE

HOMER J. TAYLOR, President

NEW YORK OFFICE, 1107 BROADWAY

Eileen Taylor, Homer J. Taylor's daughter,
circa 1906, age 5.
Crain Collection.

Eileen Taylor, age 15.
Crain Collection.

Eileen Taylor, young girl, no date.
Crain Collection.

BIBLIOGRAPHY

Barber, Edwin Atlee. *The Pottery and Porcelain of the United States* (1893 and 1901), and *Marks of American Potters* (1904). Combined edition published by Feingold & Lewis, distributed by J & J Publishing, New York, Bicentennial Limited edition.

Blake, Will T. Letter to Lucille Cox, June 7, 1938.

Boger, Louise Ade. *The Dictionary of World Pottery and Porcelain*. New York: Charles Scribner's Sons, 1971.

Boros, Ethel. "Lotus Ware, Ohio's finest," *The Plain Dealer*, August 27, 1977.

Cox, Lucille T. "This Is The Colorful Story of Lotus Ware," *East Liverpool Review*, June 16, 1938.
____. "How Isaac Knowles Rose in Pottery World," December 6, 1940.
____. "The Story of Lotus Ware," *East Palestine Daily Leader*, January 28, 1952.

Crain, Chris. Correspondence with Mary Frank Gaston, 1994.

DeBolt, Gerald. *Dictionary of American Pottery Marks*. Paducah, Kentucky: Collector Books, 1994.

Evans, Paul. "K.T.K. in California, The Homer Knowles Pottery," *Spinning Wheel*, January/February, 1978.

Frelinghuysen, Alice Cooney. "American Porcelain —1770–1920," *Metropolitan Museum of Art*. New York: Henry N. Abrams, 1989.

Gaston, Mary Frank. *American Belleek*. Paducah, Kentucky: Collector Books, 1984.
____. "American Belleek," *The Antique Trader Price Guide to Antiques*, Spring, 1988.

Gates, William C., Jr. *The City of Hills & Kilns*. East Liverpool, Ohio: The East Liverpool Historical Society, 1984.
____. "You're The Curator," *Ohio Historical Society Preview*, Spring, 1992.

Gates, William C., Jr. and Dana E. Ormerod. *The East Liverpool, Ohio, Pottery District Identification of Manufacturers and Marks*. California, Pennsylvania: The Society of Archaeology, 1982.

History of Columbiana County, Ohio. Philadelphia: D. W. Ensign & Co., J. B. Lippincott & Co. Press, 1879.

Kearns, Timothy J. *Knowles, Taylor & Knowles American Bone China*. Atglen, Pennsylvania: Schiffer Publishing Ltd., 1994.
____. "K. T. K. China Jugs Stimulated Whiskey Sales," *Antique Weekly* Vol. 27, No. 6, May 2, 1994.

Kovel, Ralph & Terry. *Kovel's New Dictionary of Marks*. New York: Crown Publishers, Inc., 1986.

Lehner, Lois. *Ohio Pottery and Glass Marks and Manufacturers*. Des Moines, Iowa: Wallace-Homestead Book Co., 1978.
____. *Lehner's Encyclopedia of U. S. Marks on Pottery, Porcelain & Clay*. Paducah, Kentucky: Collector Books, 1988.

McCord, William B. (ed. and comp.). *History of Columbiana County, Ohio and Representative Citizens*. Chicago, Illinois: Biographical Publishing Co., 1905.

Miller, Fred. "Lotus Blooms Again," *The Evening Review*, East Liverpool, Ohio, June 7, 1985.

"Ohio's Lotus Ware Popular Nationwide," *Echoes*, Ohio Historical Society, Number 8, August, 1989.

Paris, Jay. "To Smithereens," *Ohio Magazine*, Vol. 12, No. 12, March, 1990.

Popp, Robert. "Better Than Medicine!" *The Evening Review*, East Liverpool, Ohio, January 20, 1973.

Robinson, Dorothy & Bill Feeny. *The Official Price Guide to American Pottery & Porcelain*. Orlando, Florida: House of Collectibles, 1980.

Schroeder's Antiques Price Guide. Paducah, Kentucky: Collector Books, 1995.

Souvenir booklet for Knowles, Taylor & Knowles Co. East Liverpool, Ohio: F. M. Roberts Co., n.d.

Sullivan, Jack. "K.T.&K. Whiskey Jugs," *Antique Bottle and Glass Collector*, 1990.

"Wolf's Auction Americana Collection," *The Antique Trader Weekly*, March 13, 1991.

Schroeder's
ANTIQUES
Price Guide

. . . is the #1 best-selling antiques & collectibles value guide on the market today, and here's why . . .

Schroeder's ANTIQUES Price Guide

OUR #1 BEST SELLER!

Identification & Values Of Over 50,000 Antiques & Collectibles

8½ x 11, 608 Pages, $14.95

• More than 300 advisors, well-known dealers, and top-notch collectors work together with our editors to bring you accurate information regarding pricing and identification.

• More than 45,000 items in almost 500 categories are listed along with hundreds of sharp original photos that illustrate not only the rare and unusual, but the common, popular collectibles as well.

• Each large close-up shot shows important details clearly. Every subject is represented with histories and background information, a feature not found in any of our competitors' publications.

• Our editors keep abreast of newly developing trends, often adding several new categories a year as the need arises.

If it merits the interest of today's collector, you'll find it in *Schroeder's*. And you can feel confident that the information we publish is up to date and accurate. Our advisors thoroughly check each category to spot inconsistencies, listings that may not be entirely reflective of market dealings, and lines too vague to be of merit. Only the best of the lot remains for publication.

Without doubt, you'll find
SCHROEDER'S ANTIQUES PRICE GUIDE
the only one to buy for
reliable information and values.

COLLECTOR BOOKS
A Division of Schroeder Publishing Co., Inc.